PUB QUIZ

Over 2000 general
knowledge questions

Collins

HarperCollinsPublishers
Westerhill Road, Bishopbriggs
Glasgow G64 2QT

The Collins website is www.collins.co.uk

Collins Quiz Book first published 1996
Second Collins Quiz Book first published 1998
This compilation first published 2004

© HarperCollinsPublishers 2004

2

ISBN 978-0-00-780785-7

A catalogue record for this book is available from the British Library

Printed and bound in Great Britain by
Clays Ltd, St Ives plc

CONTENTS

HOW TO USE THIS BOOK

Collins Pub Quiz is simply designed and easy to use.

QUESTIONS
Each of the pages has a set of questions covering aspects of popular knowledge and culture. Ten of the questions fall into specific categories, while the eleventh in each set, the 'True or False?' question, can be used either as a tie-breaker or just as a regular question.

ANSWERS
The answers page-number for each set is flagged at the foot of its questions page. In some answers, especially in the 'True or False?' category, part of the answer appears in brackets. This is simply given as extra information and is not essential to answer the question correctly – although you can use it that way, if you want to give your quiz a harder edge.

Have fun with the questions, and good luck!

SECTION ONE

THE QUIZ BOOK QUESTIONS

SETS 1 – 240

Food & Drink

What did Snow White's wicked stepmother use to tempt her?

Natural World

What is Bovine Spongiform Encephalopathy more commonly known as?

History

How many of Henry VIII's wives lost their heads?

Culture & Belief

If a god was Cupid in Rome, what could he expect to be called in Greece?

Stage & Screen

How many different centuries did Edmund Blackadder appear in?

Written Word

In what town did Roy of the Rovers play football?

Music

On what road did Nellie the Elephant meet the head of the herd?

Famous People

The 1956 marriage of what two seeming opposites prompted the headline 'Egghead marries Hourglass'?

Sport & Leisure

Why would you be given a green jacket and a yellow jersey?

Science & Tech

What world-renowned scientist played himself in an episode of *Star Trek: The Next Generation*?

True or False?

The American inventor of the deep-freezing process was a Mr Birdseye; true or false?

ANSWERS: PAGE 251

Food & Drink What did the Israelites eat in the desert?

Natural World How high is an equine hand?

History What Roman Emperor made his horse a senator?

Culture & Belief Whose New Look caused a sensation in post-war fashion?

Stage & Screen The folk tune *Johnny Todd* was the theme music to what ground-breaking British cop drama of the 1960s?

Written Word What classic English work of literature features The Summoner, The Man Of Law and The Wife Of Bath?

Music Whose *Song of Joy* is the anthem of the European Union?

Famous People What famous sleuth contracted gangrene from biting his tongue after stumbling on an uneven pavement?

Sport & Leisure In what town do Raith Rovers play?

Science & Tech What famous motor manufacturer invented the motor car?

True or False? Sideburns were named after a prominent wearer, US Civil War General Ambrose E. Burnside; true or false?

ANSWERS: PAGE 251

Food & Drink
The berries of what shrub-like plant are used to make gin?

Natural World
What is the Windy City?

History
Why did the royal family move from Saxe-Coburg to Windsor?

Culture & Belief
Where did Panama hats originate?

Stage & Screen
In the climax of what film does the male lead climb down the presidential faces at Mount Rushmore?

Written Word
Who wrote *Look Back In Anger*?

Music
Who wrote *Don't Look Back In Anger*?

Famous People
Whose journeys aboard *The Beagle* allowed some revolutionary theories to evolve?

Sport & Leisure
What BBC TV programme popularised snooker as a spectator sport?

Science & Tech
Where would you find a Plimsoll Line?

True or False?
Scotland Yard was originally the name of a medieval house used by Scots kings visiting London; true or false?

ANSWERS: PAGE 252

Food & Drink
What did Jack Sprat refuse to eat?

Natural World
What desert separates Egypt and Israel?

History
For how long did the Berlin Wall stand?

Culture & Belief
What are the Society of Friends more commonly known as?

Stage & Screen
What was the first full-length animated feature film?

Written Word
Who are Michael, Gabriel, Uriel and Raphael?

Music
Who, according to the Stranglers, 'got an ice-pick that made his ears burn'?

Famous People
What Australian Prime Minister was said to have tweaked the Queen's bra-strap?

Sport & Leisure
What country was home to Sir Edmund Hillary?

Science & Tech
Whose relatively famous theorem had the formula $E = MC^2$?

True or False?
The Oxford–Cambridge University Boat Race has never ended in a dead heat; true or false?

ANSWERS: PAGE 252

Food & Drink What is Port Salut?

 Natural World What are the aurora borealis also known as?

 History How many Elizabeths reigned as queen in Scotland before Elizabeth II?

 Culture & Belief What God-given gift did Moses receive at Mount Sinai?

 Stage & Screen Who played Moses in the 1956 film *The Ten Commandments*?

 Written Word What Irish politician wrote a spy novel called *The Riddle Of The Sands*?

 Music What are 'Hammersmith Palais, the Bolshoi Ballet, jump back in the alley and nanny goats'?

 Famous People What business, apart from the movies, did Howard Hughes make his millions in?

 Sport & Leisure What was the official name of the original World Cup?

 Science & Tech What was the first British jet airliner?

 True or False? The first non-white British MP was elected over 100 years ago; true or false?

ANSWERS: PAGE 253

Food & Drink
What classic ad featured an alien family laughing at a traditional Earth recipe?

Natural World
If the aurora borealis are the northern lights, what are the southern lights called?

History
How many amendments have there been to the US Constitution?

Culture & Belief
What would a Scotsman tell an Englishman to do with a quaich?

Stage & Screen
What is Bollywood?

Written Word
What miser lost his gold but found a treasure in his adopted child?

Music
Whose daughter was *My Darling Clementine*?

Famous People
What did Oscar Wilde consider to be the curse of the drinking classes?

Sport & Leisure
In what year did Mark Spitz win several Olympic swimming golds?

Science & Tech
What explosive device was invented by Alfred B. Nobel, founder of the Nobel Peace Prize?

True or False?
The Queen holds UK passport number 1; true or false?

ANSWERS: PAGE 253

Food & Drink
What is the ingredient which turns curry yellow?

 Natural World
What natural feature is common to Tanzania, Uganda, Sudan and Egypt?

 History
Who was killed on the Ides of March?

 Culture & Belief
What date is the Ides of March?

 Stage & Screen
Whose undersea world was visited by *Calypso*?

 Written Word
Who did Hamlet tell to get to a nunnery?

 Music
What two 1950s pop stars died in the same plane crash as Buddy Holly?

 Famous People
What famous divorcée once declared 'One can never be too rich or too thin'?

 Sport & Leisure
In what events did Jesse Owens win his four gold medals in the 1936 Berlin Olympics?

 Science & Tech
Who invented the aqualung?

 True or False?
More people were killed in the 1906 San Francisco earthquake than on the *Titanic* in 1912; true or false?

ANSWERS: PAGE 254

Food & Drink
What inhabitants of British waters are called the Silver Darlings?

Natural World
What name was given to the Quaker William Penn's woods on the American east coast?

History
What city saw the assassination that sparked the First World War?

Culture & Belief
What would Jesus' astrological birthsign have been?

Stage & Screen
What pink piggy pals first hit British TV screens in 1957?

Written Word
Whose partner was Jacob Marley?

Music
Who was the Beatles' first drummer?

Famous People
Who said 'I love Mickey Mouse more than any woman I've ever known'?

Sport & Leisure
What Lord was the famous cricket ground named after?

Science & Tech
What is found on the Periodic Table?

True or False?
Humphrey Bogart never said 'Play it again, Sam' in *Casablanca*; true or false?

ANSWERS: PAGE 254

Food & Drink
If it's heavy in Scotland, what is it in England?

 Natural World
What is catgut traditionally made from?

 History
Who foresaw his country's civil war in the phrase 'A house divided against itself cannot stand'?

 Culture & Belief
What is bogyphobia a fear of?

 Stage & Screen
Name three of the Tracey brothers from *Thunderbirds*.

 Written Word
What was the name of Sherlock Holmes' smarter brother?

 Music
What song opened the first live broadcast of Radio 1 in 1967?

 Famous People
How did Mahatma Gandhi, Indira Gandhi and Rajiv Gandhi die?

 Sport & Leisure
Where is kabbadi most frequently played?

 Science & Tech
What British classic first went on sale in 1959 costing £496 19s 2d?

 True or False?
A granny, a sheepshank and a bowline are all parts of a chimney; true or false?

ANSWERS: PAGE 255

Food & Drink
What do you get if you boil sheep's offal, oats, suet and spices in a sheep's stomach bag?

Natural World
What deer is not actually a deer but a member of the caribou family?

History
What year saw slavery officially ended in the USA, to within five years?

Culture & Belief
What European head of state wears a crown but is not a monarch?

Stage & Screen
Who starred in a biopic of US husband-and-wife dance team Vernon and Irene Castle?

Written Word
Whose seductive dance before King Herod was rewarded with the head of John the Baptist?

Music
What American state is the home of country-and-western music?

Famous People
What did Leonardo da Vinci, Jack the Ripper and Horatio Nelson have in common?

Sport & Leisure
What are the chances of throwing a double-six with two dice?

Science & Tech
What is the seventh planet from the Sun?

True or False?
There are six counties in the province of Ulster; true or false?

ANSWERS: PAGE 255

Food & Drink
What two foods originate in the Italian town of Parma?

 Natural World
What is a shooting star?

 History
What, founded in 330 BC, was the world's first state-funded scientific institution?

 Culture & Belief
How much money would you gamble if you bet a brace of ponies?

 Stage & Screen
What four-legged companion went with Dorothy from Kansas to Oz?

 Written Word
If the *Times* came from London and the *Herald* from Glasgow, where did the *Guardian* come from?

 Music
'Satchmo' was the nickname of what jazz legend?

 Famous People
What is the name 'Satchmo' short for?

Sport & Leisure
Who said in 1966, 'They think it's all over – it is now'?

Science & Tech.
How did Valentina Tereshkova shoot to fame in 1963?

 True or False?
James VI of Scotland and I of England wrote an anti-smoking tract in 1604; true or false?

ANSWERS: PAGE 256

Food & Drink
What did a million housewives say every day in the 1970s?

 Natural World
What is the world's longest river?

 History
Who was the first woman ever elected to the British Parliament?

 Culture & Belief
Who is the patron saint of lovers?

 Stage & Screen
What two actors have refused their Oscars?

 Written Word
Who was the Fat Owl of the Remove?

 Music
What chart-topping 1980s band was named after a family friend of Mr Spock?

 Famous People
Who ruled longest – Queen Victoria or Louis XIV of France?

 Sport & Leisure
Who won snooker's 1985 world championship with the last ball of the final game?

 Science & Tech
What is the world's longest single-span suspension bridge?

 True or False?
Tupperware was invented by Mr Tupper; true or false?

ANSWERS: PAGE 256

Food & Drink
What is the Greek pastry baklava sweetened with?

Natural World
What is the world's second-highest mountain?

History
What happened at 11:00 a.m. on 11 November, 1918?

Culture & Belief
How many years would you be married if you were celebrating your tin wedding anniversary?

Stage & Screen
Whose screen test reported 'Can't act, can't sing, slightly bald. Can dance a little'?

Written Word
Who was Graham Greene's *Third Man*?

Music
What was the opening song of the Live Aid concert at Wembley Stadium in July 1985?

Famous People
Whose 1938 radio production of *War of The Worlds* had thousands of Americans fleeing invading Martians?

Sport & Leisure
Who won football's first World Cup?

Science & Tech
What US politician was the first American to orbit the Earth?

True or False?
Bagpipers run the risk of lung infections from bacteria which lurk inside their bags; true or false?

ANSWERS: PAGE 257

Food & Drink
What is the main ingredient in Palestine soup?

 Natural World
What are Bailey, Malin and German Bight?

 History
What scholarly monarch was called 'the wisest fool in Christendom'?

 Culture & Belief
What does 'amen' mean?

 Stage & Screen
Who had a *Brief Encounter*?

 Written Word
Who created *The Simpsons*?

 Music
What famous Irish folk band did James Galway and Van Morrison record hit albums with?

 Famous People
Where was Thomas à Becket murdered?

 Sport & Leisure
What board game, invented in 1931, was first called Criss-Cross?

 Science & Tech
How long, to the nearest minute, does sunlight take to reach the Earth?

 True or False?
Adolf Hitler used his grandmother's name of Schicklgruber for several years; true or false?

ANSWERS: PAGE 257

Food & Drink
Where would an American put a weenie?

 Natural World
What American state has the nickname 'the Lone Star State'?

 History
Who was the shortest-reigning English monarch?

 Culture & Belief
What is the Muslim holy book called?

 Stage & Screen
What was the birthday of George M. Cohan's *Yankee Doodle Dandy*?

 Written Word
Who is older, Superman or Batman?

 Music
What was the name of Elvis Presley's original backing band?

 Famous People
What person was said to be the inspiration and namesake of the teddy bear?

 Sport & Leisure
What would you use to play chemin de fer?

 Science & Tech
If you had a painful patella, which part of your body would hurt?

 True or False?
Adolf Hitler was a trained housepainter; true or false?

ANSWERS: PAGE 258

Food & Drink What drink taught the world to sing in the 1970s?

 Natural World What is the capital of Australia?

 History Which side fired the first shot in the American Civil War?

 Culture & Belief What was the only thing that remained in Pandora's Box?

 Stage & Screen What cult 1980s film had *Man In Motion* by John Parr as its theme?

 Written Word What was Superman's original home town called?

 Music Who was the most-played composer at the Proms – Elgar, Wagner or Beethoven?

 Famous People Who was the original millionaire philanthropist who built and owned Skibo Castle in Sutherland?

 Sport & Leisure In which sport would you encounter a jerk?

 Science & Tech What is deoxyribonucleic acid better known as?

 True or False? Margaret Thatcher was a member of the Labour Party for almost two years in her youth; true or false?

ANSWERS: PAGE 258

Food & Drink
What would you find in the middle of a Sussex Pond Pudding?

Natural World
What is the world's largest island (excluding the continents)?

History
How many Jameses were kings of Scots?

Culture & Belief
What date was Jesus conceived on?

Stage & Screen
What 1960s children's TV show featured Vienna's Lippizaner horses?

Written Word
Who is Eric Blair better known as?

Music
What did Judy Collins have in common with the Royal Scots Dragoon Guards?

Famous People
What European leader used his presidential powers to check a takeover of his favourite brewery?

Sport & Leisure
Which two teams met in the world's first international football fixture?

Science & Tech
What elementary discovery was made by Crick and Watson?

True or False?
Sumer is Icumen In, from the 13th century, is the earliest known musical canon; true or false?

ANSWERS: PAGE 259

Food & Drink
Who was said to have advised starving French citizens to eat cake?

 Natural World
What city, which is a country, is the world's smallest?

 History
Where was the Crystal Palace originally built?

 Culture & Belief
What religion believes in the balance of Yin and Yang?

 Stage & Screen
'As if by magic, the shopkeeper appeared' in what TV show?

 Written Word
Who was Charles Dodgson better known as?

 Music
What city was Maria Callas' birthplace?

 Famous People
Who said, 'In the future everyone will be world-famous for fifteen minutes'?

 Sport & Leisure
What does the TT in motorcycling's TT Races stand for?

 Science & Tech
What process, first used to preserve wine, now preserves milk?

 True or False?
Leonardo da Vinci sculpted the *Venus de Milo*; true or false?

ANSWERS: PAGE 259

Food & Drink What drink is known as uisge beatha (pronounced 'ooskay baa'), meaning the water of life?

 Natural World What country uses the zloty as currency?

 History What event was the Crystal Palace built to house?

 Culture & Belief What church recruits unwitting followers through posthumous baptism ceremonies?

 Stage & Screen What town is Coronation Street in?

 Written Word What writer turned down a peerage and the Order of Merit but accepted the Nobel Prize for Literature?

 Music Who urged his listeners to *Keep Right On To The End Of The Road*?

 Famous People Who was the second man to walk on the moon?

 Sport & Leisure Who was Britain's first million-pound footballer?

 Science & Tech What do the saxophone, the guillotine and the biro pen have in common?

 True or False? Until the 19th century, Italian boy sopranos could be castrated to preserve their high voices; true or false?

ANSWERS: PAGE 260

Food & Drink
In what concoctions were the victims of serial killer Sweeney Todd said to have ended up?

 Natural World
What is the difference between a leopard and a panther?

 History
Who was the only US president to have been elected four times?

 Culture & Belief
What name was Ras Tafari better known by?

 Stage & Screen
What famous family lives in Ambridge?

 Written Word
What was Dale Carnegie's most winning and influential book?

 Music
Who lost her heart to a starship trooper in 1978?

 Famous People
What famous Crimea veteran was 'the lady with the lamp'?

 Sport & Leisure
How long does a 12-round boxing match last if it goes the full distance?

 Science & Tech
What number would an ancient Roman write as MI?

 True or False?
William Shakespeare wrote *Hamlet* as anti-Danish propaganda while England and Denmark were at war; true or false?

ANSWERS: PAGE 260

Food & Drink
What is the vegetable Americans call an eggplant known as in Britain?

Natural World
What makes a humming bird hum?

History
Who was the second Lord Protector of England, Scotland and Ireland?

Culture & Belief
What religion reveres the god Krishna?

Stage & Screen
What was the name of Powell and Pressburger's film production company?

Written Word
Who did Gore Vidal call 'the Acting President'?

Music
What conductor got classical music in Birmingham all shook up?

Famous People
What politician was called 'the Uncrowned King of Ireland'?

Sport & Leisure
At which Olympics did synchronised swimming first appear?

Science & Tech
What is iron oxide more commonly known as?

True or False?
English is the world's most-spoken language; true or false?

ANSWERS: PAGE 261

Food & Drink
What drink is produced around the Spanish town of Jerez?

 Natural World
Roughly how many species of insect are there in Britain – 1000, 10,000, 20,000, 30,000?

 History
What is King John said to have lost in The Wash?

 Culture & Belief
What is the only surviving wonder of the ancient world?

 Stage & Screen
What time-travelling medieval wizard was dazzled by electrickery and the telling-bone?

 Written Word
In what street would you find Smiffy, Wilfrid, Danny and Plug?

 Music
What were the boys of NYPD choir singing in *The Fairytale Of New York*?

 Famous People
Who was first to reach the South Pole?

 Sport & Leisure
What baseball player made at least one hit in each of 56 successive games in 1941?

 Science & Tech
How many degrees do complementary angles make up?

True or False?
The vacuum cleaner was invented by a Mr Hoover; true or false?

ANSWERS: PAGE 261

Food & Drink

What is a calzone?

 Natural World

What city could you look down on from Table Mountain?

 History

What did Nelson lose at Tenerife?

 Culture & Belief

What would you be studying if your subject was sinology?

 Stage & Screen

What soap set in Spain failed to strike gold?

 Written Word

What famous family lived at 50 Wimpole Street, London?

 Music

What is the term for a group of seven performing musicians?

 Famous People

What psychic shot to fame by repairing watches and breaking cutlery?

 Sport & Leisure

Who was the first unseeded player to win the men's singles at Wimbledon?

 Science & Tech

When, to the nearest three years, did the first daily air service between Paris and London begin?

 True or False?

Snotra was the Norse god of Wisdom; true or false?

ANSWERS: PAGE 262

Food & Drink
What writer collapsed and died while mixing a mayonnaise?

Natural World
What would you be doing if you were playing possum?

History
Who was the last emperor of India?

Culture & Belief
Where in a church would you find a nave?

Stage & Screen
Where could Peter the Postman, Dr Mopp, Windy Miller and PC McGarry be found in the 1960s?

Written Word
What Irish-born writer created the land of Narnia?

Music
Who took the Lennon-McCartney song *Michelle* to number one in the UK charts?

Famous People
What revered all-American hero joined the Boston Tea Party and rode to warn of the arrival of the British?

Sport & Leisure
What Irish writer was the only Nobel Prizewinner ever to be listed in Wisden's *Cricketer's Almanac*?

Science & Tech
What chemical element is represented by He on the Periodic Table?

True or False?
Catholicism is the world's largest religion; true or false?

ANSWERS: PAGE 262

Food & Drink — What is the main ingredient boxty, colcannon and champ have in common?

 Natural World — What is the world's biggest baby?

 History — On what date did the USA celebrate its bicentennial?

 Culture & Belief — Who was the first person to be killed in the Bible?

 Stage & Screen — What Nobel-prize-winning dramatist had a *Long Day's Journey into Night*?

 Written Word — What First World War poet wrote an *Anthem For Doomed Youth*?

 Music — Who thought in 1977 that *Red Light Spells Danger*?

 Famous People — Who claimed she lost her virginity as a career move?

 Sport & Leisure — What Caribbean country entered a bobsleigh team in the 1988 Winter Olympics?

 Science & Tech — What innovation in sound recording was invented in 1978?

 True or False? — The century plant blooms only once a century; true or false?

What is scampi made from?

 What city was previously known as Byzantium and Constantinople?

 Who were 'overpaid, oversexed and over here'?

 What Israeli king did both Donatello and Michelangelo sculpt?

 What two antipodean wonders spoke in a language humans could understand?

 What is the name of Dennis the Menace's dog?

 What kilted singer asked *Donald, Where's Yer Troosers*?

 Who declared 'I can resist everything except temptation'?

 What city hosted the first Olympic Games of the modern era?

 What would you be studying if your subject was virology?

Orson Welles and Rita Hayworth were husband and wife; true or false?

ANSWERS: PAGE 263

Food & Drink
Whose divine dinners consisted of ambrosia and nectar?

Natural World
What country is Kathmandu the capital of?

History
What was the last battle fought on British soil?

Culture & Belief
Whose 1920s' ad campaign permanently changed Father Christmas' costume from green to red?

Stage & Screen
Who wrote *A Streetcar Named Desire*?

Written Word
What recollections make up the world's longest novel?

Music
What top British band used to be known as Seymour?

Famous People
What evangelical preacher supported Richard Nixon and prayed at Bill Clinton's inauguration?

Sport & Leisure
How many balls are on a snooker table at the start of a game?

Science & Tech
How many teeth does the adult human have?

True or False?
By 1996, Britain's favourite food was still fish and chips; true or false?

ANSWERS: PAGE 264

Food & Drink
What is a rollmop?

 Natural World
What is the only man-made object claimed to be visible from space?

 History
Who told the British government 'We only have to be lucky once – you will have to be lucky always'?

 Culture & Belief
Who was the son of King Uther Pendragon?

 Stage & Screen
Who feuded with the Montagues in *Romeo and Juliet*?

 Written Word
Who was *The Once and Future King*?

 Music
What former Yardbird joined Ginger Baker and Jack Bruce to form Cream?

 Famous People
What was Malcolm X's other diminutive surname?

 Sport & Leisure
What were the Commonwealth Games originally called in 1930?

 Science & Tech
What is the largest muscle in the human body?

True or False?
A Mr Singer invented the sewing machine; true or false?

ANSWERS: PAGE 264

Food & Drink
What is the sour ingredient in a whisky sour?

 Natural World
What country occupied almost one-sixth of the Earth's surface until 1991, but does not do so now?

 History
What organisation's motto translates as 'Evil Be To Him Who Evil Thinks'?

 Culture & Belief
What is Siddhartha Gautama better known as?

 Stage & Screen
What film features Holly Golightly?

 Written Word
What is the name of Noddy's best friend?

 Music
What did my true love send to me on the eighth day of Christmas?

 Famous People
Who was Harlean Carpenter better known as?

 Sport & Leisure
What was the first year that professional players were invited to Wimbledon?

 Science & Tech
How many hands does Big Ben have?

 True or False?
A giraffe has the same number of bones in its neck as a human; true or false?

ANSWERS: PAGE 265

Food & Drink Apart from appearing in the Bible, what do Balthazar, Methuselah and Nebuchadnezzar have in common?

 Natural World What would you be studying if you were a batologist?

 History When was the Prague Spring?

 Culture & Belief What does the word 'guru' mean?

 Stage & Screen Who declared his crew's intention 'to boldly go where no-one has gone before'?

 Written Word How many legs did Enid Blyton's Famous Five have altogether?

 Music Who are the Three Tenors?

 Famous People 'Kissing her was like kissing Hitler'. Who was Tony Curtis describing?

 Sport & Leisure Who was the only woman competitor at the 1976 Montreal Olympic Games not to be given a sex test?

 Science & Tech What scientist was reputedly told by his schoolteacher 'You will never amount to anything'?

 True or False? The first person recorded as describing the British weather was Julius Caesar during his invasion of 55 BC; true or false?

ANSWERS: PAGE 265

Food & Drink — What guerrilla fighter had a biscuit named after him?

 Natural World — If you had panophobia, what would you fear?

 History — What was the last state to join the American Union?

 Culture & Belief — How many languages are allowed by law to be used in adverts in France?

 Stage & Screen — Who do Father Dougal and Father Jack share the Craggy Island parochial house with?

 Written Word — The novels of what Edinburgh writer were used to name a football team and a railway station?

 Music — What Kenny Rogers song sparked a series of four TV movies?

 Famous People — What head of state did the American CIA reputedly try to assassinate with an exploding cigar?

 Sport & Leisure — Who was the first player to win the Wimbledon Men's Championship five times in a row?

 Science & Tech — What fraction is used to express pi?

 True or False? — An antimacassar was a special kind of mop used to polish Victorian tiled floors; true or false?

ANSWERS: PAGE 266

Food & Drink
What did Yogi Bear steal in Jellystone Park?

 Natural World
What is the name for a low-pressure system bringing unsettled weather?

 History
How many British popes have there been?

 Culture & Belief
What is a greenback?

 Stage & Screen
What is unusual about Commander Data in *Star Trek: The Next Generation*?

 Written Word
What is the name of Andy Capp's long-suffering wife?

 Music
What world-famous conductor was married to British cellist Jacqueline du Pré?

 Famous People
Who is the Albanian Agnes Gauxha Bojaxhiu better known as?

 Sport & Leisure
What sport was revolutionised by Dick Fosbury's flop?

 Science & Tech
Who is known as the 'father' of the atom bomb?

 True or False?
Cartoon character Popeye has a hamburger-eating friend called Wimpy; true or false?

ANSWERS: PAGE 266

Food & Drink
What made Milwaukee famous?

Natural World
What cloud types are higher – stratus or cirrus?

History
What were the members of the Women's Social and Political Union popularly known as?

Culture & Belief
Whose commercials in the 1960s encouraged you to 'Put a tiger in your tank'?

Stage & Screen
What movie set in pre-war Germany was based on Christopher Isherwood's *Goodbye to Berlin*?

Written Word
What Japanese novelist committed hara-kiri after his attempted coup failed?

Music
Would you blow, pluck or hit a bazouki?

Famous People
What month was named in honour of Roman general Gaius Julius Caesar?

Sport & Leisure
Which famous US basketball team ran on court to their theme tune, *Sweet Georgia Brown*?

Science & Tech
What is a cock-up splint used to support?

True or False?
The safety razor was invented by a Mr Gillette; true or false?

ANSWERS: PAGE 267

Food & Drink
What ballerina gave her name to an Australian pudding?

 Natural World
How far would you have to journey to get to the centre of the Earth?

 History
Who is the First Lord of the Treasury?

 Culture & Belief
What New York State farm gave its name to a landmark event of the flower-power era in 1969?

 Stage & Screen
What FBI duo believe The Truth is Out There?

 Written Word
What cartoon strip, inspiring a TV sitcom and movie, was created by Charles Addams?

 Music
What would a bagpiper do with a chanter?

 Famous People
Who was the Young Pretender?

 Sport & Leisure
What sport developed from the first Hawaii Ironman Competition in 1974?

 Science & Tech
Until 1745, what were barbers officially able to perform as well as haircuts?

 True or False?
The pound note first came into circulation during the Napoleonic Wars; true or false?

ANSWERS: PAGE 267

Food & Drink
What was John the Baptist said to have eaten in the desert?

Natural World
Arches, loops, whorls and composites are all types of what?

History
How many members were originally in the Common Market?

Culture & Belief
What saint prayed, 'Oh Lord, make me chaste, but not yet?'

Stage & Screen
What grumpy pensioner had *One Foot in the Grave*?

Written Word
What science fiction author wrote the *Earthsea* trilogy?

Music
What band topped the UK chart in 1996 with *Spaceman*?

Famous People
Whose granddaughter Patti was kidnapped by the Symbionese Liberation Army?

Sport & Leisure
In which sport would you find soling, Flying Dutchman and tornado competition classes?

Science & Tech
What temperature does water boil at on the Fahrenheit scale?

True or False?
A sponge is an animal; true or false?

ANSWERS: PAGE 268

Food & Drink What is the ingredient used to flavour Amaretto liqueurs and biscuits?

 Natural World What is the difference between lava and magma?

 History What did the Duke of Wellington describe as 'a close-run thing'?

 Culture & Belief Whose inscription in St Paul's Cathedral translates as 'If you seek a monument, look around you'?

 Stage & Screen What was experienced by the inhabitants of Cicely, Alaska?

 Written Word What recent conflict was described by an Argentinian writer as 'two bald men fighting over a comb'?

 Music Whose body lies a-mouldering in the grave while his soul goes marching on?

 Famous People Who was Anna Mae Bullock married to?

 Sport & Leisure Who is the only player to have scored a hat-trick in the World Cup final?

 Science & Tech How many stomachs does a cow have?

True or False? Mahatma Gandhi was born in South Africa; true or false?

ANSWERS: PAGE 268

Food & Drink
Mashed neeps and tatties are the traditional accompaniments to what Scots delicacy?

 Natural World
How many time zones are there in mainland USA?

 History
What were the colours of the first two British stamps?

 Culture & Belief
What American terrorist group took their name from, a line in a Bob Dylan song?

 Stage & Screen
What does *ER* stand for?

 Written Word
What novel, by a former teacher, charts the descent into savagery of boys marooned on a desert island?

 Music
What band sang about *Waterloo Sunset*?

 Famous People
What Argentinian doctor was boss of Cuba's national bank before going to Bolivia to start a revolution?

 Sport & Leisure
Where was netball invented?

 Science & Tech
If you suffered from hypotension would your blood pressure be too high or too low?

 True or False?
Patagonia is a fictitious land from the works of 18th-century satirist Jonathan Swift; true or false?

ANSWERS: PAGE 269

Food & Drink
What is the minimum age for a malt whisky?

 Natural World
What does a limnologist study?

 History
What was William the Bastard's more common nickname?

 Culture & Belief
What would a yachtsman use a burgee for?

 Stage & Screen
What was odd about the TV detective pairing of Randall and Hopkirk?

 Written Word
Where did Kubla Khan a stately pleasure-dome decree?

 Music
Who wrote the opera *Madame Butterfly*?

 Famous People
What British leader was described as 'a very big woman, terrifying to look at, with a fierce look'?

 Sport & Leisure
Which three of the five Classic horse races make up the English Triple Crown?

 Science & Tech
What is the only organ in the human body capable of regeneration?

 True or False?
A Mr Fahrenheit invented the mercury thermometer; true or false?

ANSWERS: PAGE 269

Food & Drink
What makes jelly gel?

 Natural World
How many degrees of the Earth's surface does the sun travel across in one hour?

 History
Where in Europe did King Zog rule until 1946?

 Culture & Belief
What cult was invented by American science-fiction writer L. Ron Hubbard?

 Stage & Screen
What Boston bar did Sam run, Diane work and Frasier drink in?

 Written Word
What towns were the setting for Charles Dickens' *A Tale Of Two Cities*?

 Music
What country star is the world's biggest-selling performance artist?

 Famous People
What rotund ruler merited the nickname Tum-Tum?

 Sport & Leisure
In wrestling, which is heavier, bantamweight or featherweight?

 Science & Tech
What organism in bread makes it rise?

 True or False?
Richard the Lionheart introduced the handkerchief to fashion in the 14th century; true or false?

ANSWERS: PAGE 270

Food & Drink What dish is traditionally associated with Easter?

 Natural World What do the initials a.m. and p.m. literally mean?

 History What is the world's oldest city?

 Culture & Belief What dance phenomenon had its first airing at the 1994 Eurovision Song Contest?

 Stage & Screen What group of bright young things frequented New York's Central Perk coffee bar?

 Written Word Who wrote, 'Morality is simply the attitude we adopt towards people whom we personally dislike'?

 Music What alphabetical band had a *Lexicon Of Love*?

 Famous People By what childish name was Henry McCarty later and better known?

 Sport & Leisure Which legendary golfer initiated the US Masters golf tournament?

 Science & Tech What colour would an acid turn litmus paper?

 True or False? Escapologist Harry Houdini died in a drowning accident during one of his tricks; true or false?

ANSWERS: PAGE 270

Food & Drink What did the Romans mainly use salt for?

 Natural World What are the two largest countries in the continent of Oceania?

 History What year was the halfpenny phased out?

 Culture & Belief What would you be afraid of if you suffered from papaphobia?

 Stage & Screen What house did Charles Ryder revisit in the book and 1980s TV series?

 Written Word What extraordinary book did Ford Prefect own?

 Music Who was the lead singer of Thin Lizzy?

 Famous People Who shot Billy the Kid in 1881?

 Sport & Leisure What do Hamilton in Canada, Perth in Australia and Kingston in Jamaica have in common?

 Science & Tech What metal was commonly known as quicksilver?

 True or False? Three US presidents have resigned from office; true or false?

ANSWERS: PAGE 271

Food & Drink
The Roman poet Juvenal said people only wanted two things; one was circuses. What was the other?

Natural World
What is the most abundant metal in the Earth's crust?

History
What was the ship it was claimed that God couldn't sink?

Culture & Belief
What freedom fighter said 'I want to be the white man's brother, not his brother-in-law'?

Stage & Screen
His performance in what film won John Wayne his only Oscar?

Written Word
What five things did Old King Cole call for?

Music
Who sang about *A Boy Named Sue*?

Famous People
What millionaire philanthropist once claimed, 'The man who dies rich dies disgraced'?

Sport & Leisure
Which two British cities have hosted the final of the European Cup?

Science & Tech
How many numbers are there in a binary counting system?

True or False?
Tsar Peter the Great of Russia introduced the Japanese art of flower-arranging to the West; true or false?

ANSWERS: PAGE 271

Food & Drink

What months of the year are diners advised to avoid oysters?

Natural World

What are pearls composed of?

History

In what decade did native Americans become American citizens?

Culture & Belief

How many pennies could you get to a pound before decimalisation?

Stage & Screen

Whose army recruited Private Pike, Corporal Jones and Sergeant Wilson?

Written Word

What did Solomon Grundy do on Saturday?

Music

In what song did The Who hope they died before they got old?

Famous People

Of what prime minister did Margot Asquith say 'He could never see a belt without hitting below it'?

Sport & Leisure

What sport was the subject of the bestselling book, *Rare Air*?

Science & Tech

What is the unit of measurement for pressure?

True or False?

German physicist Heinrich Hertz also co-founded the well known car-hire company; true or false?

ANSWERS: PAGE 272

Food & Drink
What is unusual about the bread traditionally eaten at Passover?

 Natural World
What are the Chinook, the Mistral and the Sirocco?

 History
Which arm did Nelson lose at the Battle of Santa Cruz?

 Culture & Belief
Who was the first Christian martyr?

 Stage & Screen
What British TV first was achieved by *Stingray*?

 Written Word
What do seven magpies signify?

 Music
What band asked *Do You Really Want To Hurt Me?* in 1982?

 Famous People
Who made his fortune in the US with nickel-and-dime stores?

 Sport & Leisure
What trophy did the Wanderers and the Royal Engineers contest for the first time in 1872?

 Science & Tech
If you travelled at Mach 2, how fast would you be going?

 True or False?
Leon Trotsky was born in Dublin's Jewish district and taken to the Ukraine by his parents as a baby; true or false?

ANSWERS: PAGE 272

Food & Drink

What Biblical character spent three days and nights as fish food?

 Natural World

What American state is Juneau the capital of?

 History

Who was the USA's first Catholic president?

 Culture & Belief

What two brothers with a talent for promotion coined the phrase 'Labour Isn't Working' in 1978?

 Stage & Screen

Who did King Kong fall for in the 1933 movie?

 Written Word

What was the significance of *Fahrenheit 451*?

 Music

What chart-topping duo did Vince Clark form after he left Yazoo?

 Famous People

What US president's previous jobs included that of male model?

 Sport & Leisure

Which is the fastest of all ball games?

 Science & Tech

How many degrees' difference is there between 0° Centigrade and 0° Kelvin, to the nearest 10°?

 True or False?

Allan Pinkerton, founder of the famous American detective agency, was a Glaswegian; true or false?

ANSWERS: PAGE 273

Food & Drink
What is unusual about the meat served in steak tartare?

Natural World
If the Greenwich meridian is at 0 degrees, what is at 180 degrees?

History
What was Al Capone eventually imprisoned for?

Culture & Belief
What type of clothing takes its name from an island in Shetland?

Stage & Screen
What cult 1960s show featured TV's first inter-racial kiss?

Written Word
What did Robert Burns address as the 'Great chieftain o' the puddin'-race'?

Music
Name one of the two acts who have had a hit with *La Bamba*?

Famous People
What was the nickname of Manfred von Richthofen, the First World War's most successful pilot?

Sport & Leisure
Over how many holes is the British Open golf tournament contested?

Science & Tech
What is combined with copper to create bronze?

True or False?
In the past, carrots were white, purple and yellow, but not orange; true or false?

ANSWERS: PAGE 273

Food & Drink
What dish is known as a London particular?

Natural World
What meteorological phenomenon did Charles Dickens call a London particular?

History
Who was the victor of the Battle of the Little Bighorn?

Culture & Belief
What are quasi-non-governmental organisations better known as?

Stage & Screen
What was the name of the Lone Ranger's horse?

Written Word
How many of the Brontë sisters were published authors?

Music
What is the term for singing without any musical accompaniment?

Famous People
What would Napoleon have found it almost impossible to do tonight, or any other night, in bed?

Sport & Leisure
The governing body of which sport has its headquarters at Hurlingham in London?

Science & Tech
Which is heavier, an imperial ton or a metric tonne?

True or False?
Laws were passed in Elizabethan England to prevent commoners and peasants wearing hats; true or false?

ANSWERS: PAGE 274

Food & Drink

What is the main ingredient of laver soup?

Natural World

When is Halley's Comet next due to pass near Earth?

History

What nation was the first to use concentration camps?

Culture & Belief

Where would you find the Book of Habakkuk?

Stage & Screen

What was the title of Mickey Mouse's first celluloid outing?

Written Word

What dramatist claimed that if there were no anti-Semitism he would not think of himself as Jewish?

Music

Who had most hits simultaneously in the UK Top 30?

Famous People

What monarch was officially insane for the last nine years of his reign?

Sport & Leisure

Which runner held world records simultaneously at 1500 m, 2000 m, 3000 m and 5000 m in 1990?

Science & Tech

What natural phenomenon would a seismograph record?

True or False?

The cylinder lock was invented by a Mr Yale; true or false?

ANSWERS: PAGE 274

Food & Drink
Where did chilli con carne originate?

 Natural World
What is the most populous native American tribe in the USA?

 History
What was reportedly seen at Roswell, New Mexico, in July, 1947?

 Culture & Belief
What does the word 'terracotta' mean?

 Stage & Screen
What was the name of *The Godfather's* Sicilian home village?

 Written Word
Who wrote *The Playboy Of The Western World*?

 Music
What spiritual song was the anthem of the 1960s' American Civil Rights Movement?

 Famous People
Who ate poisoned cakes and was shot twice but only died after being tied up and thrown in a river?

 Sport & Leisure
What sport was introduced to Britain in 1867 by a party of Caughnawaga Indians from Canada?

 Science & Tech
If you knew your humerus from your gluteus maximus, what parts of your body could you identify?

 True or False?
Writer Aldous Huxley taught George Orwell at Eton; true or false?

ANSWERS: PAGE 275

Food & Drink
What, according to Dr Johnson, was eaten by horses in England and people in Scotland?

Natural World
What is the world's highest waterfall?

History
Which Robert do Bobbies take their name from?

Culture & Belief
What would an American keep in his billfold?

Stage & Screen
What is the family relationship between Francis Ford Coppola and Nicholas Cage?

Written Word
Who wrote *The Godfather*?

Music
What in the First World War went ting-a-ling-a-ling for you but not for me?

Famous People
Who was T. E. Lawrence better known as?

Sport & Leisure
What is the exact imperial distance of a marathon race?

Science & Tech
What size are the internal angles of an equilateral triangle?

True or False?
Water drains down plugholes clockwise in the Southern Hemisphere; true or false?

ANSWERS: PAGE 275

Food & Drink
What, until the BSE scare, was Desperate Dan's favourite food?

Natural World
What mammal's pregnancies last longer than any other on earth?

History
What do the initials 'G.I.' stand for?

Culture & Belief
What saint is represented by the emblem of a shower of rain?

Stage & Screen
What classic British wartime drama won two Oscars for its star and creator, Noël Coward?

Written Word
What writer said 'Other people have a nationality. The Irish and the Jews have a psychosis'?

Music
What is an aria in an opera?

Famous People
What fashion designer first came to prominence with her bondage wear during the punk era?

Sport & Leisure
What weapon is used in the Japanese martial art of kendo?

Science & Tech
Why is ethylene glycol added to car engines?

True or False?
Scotch whisky is also produced in Japan; true or false?

ANSWERS: PAGE 276

Food & Drink

What, according to the nursery rhyme, are little girls made of?

 Natural World

What country used to be called Siam?

 History

Where did the Boxer Rising take place?

 Culture & Belief

What does a Bat Mitzvah mark in the Jewish faith?

 Stage & Screen

What film featured *Lara's Theme*?

 Written Word

Who is credited with writing *Auld Lang Syne*?

 Music

What opera is Bizet's most famous and popular?

 Famous People

Who offered motor-car buyers any colour they liked, so long as it was black?

 Sport & Leisure

What type of surface would a bandy match be played on?

 Science & Tech

Which is longer, a nautical mile or a terrestrial mile?

 True or False?

A dodecagon was a carnivorous dinosaur; true or false?

ANSWERS: PAGE 276

Food & Drink

In what decade did sliced bread first appear?

Natural World

What causes the tides?

History

What fleet-footed IRA kidnap victim from the 1980s was never seen again?

Culture & Belief

Which of the 12 apostles was the tax-collector?

Stage & Screen

What film had *Moon River* as its theme music?

Written Word

What cartoon-strip family comprises Homer, Marge, Lisa, Bart and Maggie?

Music

Who were *Pretty Vacant* in 1977?

Famous People

What two historic martial heroes guard the gateway to Edinburgh Castle?

Sport & Leisure

How many fences are there in the Aintree Grand National?

Science & Tech

How many ounces are there in a kilogram, approximately?

True or False?

Kr is the symbol used to represent the element Krypton in the Periodic Table; true or false?

ANSWERS: PAGE 277

Food & Drink
What biscuit did West Country physician Dr William Oliver give his name to?

Natural World
How much skin is on the average adult male body, to the nearest square foot?

History
When was the United Kingdom founded?

Culture & Belief
What did the East End Revival Society become in 1878?

Stage & Screen
What orchestra played the theme to 1970s Dutch cop drama *Van Der Valk*?

Written Word
Who is credited with writing *The Iliad* and *The Odyssey*?

Music
What famous West End musical is based on a collection of children's poems by T. S. Eliot?

Famous People
What utilitarian philosopher espoused the greatest happiness for the greatest number?

Sport & Leisure
Which US city plays host to the world's oldest annual marathon?

Science & Tech
How many litres of air does a fit adult take in with each breath?

True or False?
The lawnmower was invented by a Mr Budding; true or false?

ANSWERS: PAGE 277

What prime minister's last words were 'I think I could eat one of Bellamy's veal pies'?

 How many countries are there in Great Britain?

 What three Queens had Glasgow as their first home town?

 What item of fashion did Mary Quant invent?

 What military rank did James Bond hold?

 Who wrote *Ulysses*?

 Whose album *Arrival* topped the UK charts in 1977?

 Who was manager of Manchester United at the time of the Munich Air Disaster?

 Which is the oldest of the English Classic horse races?

 What does vulcanisation do to rubber?

New York boasted the world's first skyscraper; true or false?

ANSWERS: PAGE 278

Food & Drink — What British necessity did J.B. Priestley describe as 'the slow revenge of the Orient'?

Natural World — How many inhabited Channel Islands are there?

History — What does the monarch traditionally distribute on Maundy Thursday?

Culture & Belief — What does etcetera mean?

Stage & Screen — What rock star played a teacher in the film *Back to the Future*?

Written Word — What English poet penned *The Mask Of Anarchy*?

Music — What pianist and composer was the King of Ragtime music?

Famous People — Who was the Irish-American choreography genius behind the Riverdance phenomenon?

Sport & Leisure — What game is played on a diamond?

Science & Tech — What was the invention which allowed multi-storey buildings to be built?

True or False? — Chimpanzees are more closely related to humans than to gorillas; true or false?

ANSWERS: PAGE 278

Food & Drink What would you traditionally cook tandoori chicken in?

 Natural World What is England's highest mountain?

 History What practice did former PM Harold Macmillan describe as 'selling the family silver'?

 Culture & Belief Where in a car would Americans store their luggage?

 Stage & Screen What was the stage name of Marion Morrison?

 Written Word What philosopher was Alexander the Great's teacher?

 Music What famous West End musical is based on the opera *Madame Butterfly*?

 Famous People Who urged the hippy generation to 'Turn on, tune in, drop out'?

 Sport & Leisure At which course is the Derby run each year?

 Science & Tech What vitamin deficiency causes scurvy?

 True or False? Baden-Powell started the Girl Guide movement as well as the Boy Scouts; true or false?

ANSWERS: PAGE 279

Food & Drink

To what favourite British dish are sodium chloride and acetic acid common additives?

 Natural World

What are the four provinces of Ireland?

 History

Who was shot and seriously wounded in Dallas, Texas on 22 November 1963?

 Culture & Belief

What is the Book of the Apocalypse better known as?

 Stage & Screen

Which of Marilyn Monroe's films ended with her version of *I Want To Be Loved By You*?

 Written Word

What British politician wrote *A History Of The English-Speaking Peoples*?

 Music

What performing company was most closely associated with the work of Gilbert and Sullivan?

 Famous People

What future prime minister declared, after winning a primary school prize, 'I wasn't lucky. I deserved it'?

 Sport & Leisure

The Colts football team and the Orioles baseball team are based in which US city?

 Science & Tech

What did the Royal Navy formerly carry on its ships to counteract scurvy in the crew?

 True or False?

Museum visitors in cultural centres such as Florence often contract Stendhal's Syndrome, a form of art fatigue; true or false?

ANSWERS: PAGE 279

Food & Drink — How many legs has a Bombay Duck?

 Natural World — What is the second-biggest city in Ireland?

 History — What was nicknamed 'The Iron Horse'?

 Culture & Belief — Who painted *The Laughing Cavalier*?

 Stage & Screen — In what film did Sherlock Holmes pursue Jack the Ripper through an establishment masonic conspiracy?

 Written Word — What Shakespearean play is the musical *Kiss Me, Kate* based on?

 Music — What was Abba's last UK number 1 hit?

 Famous People — What Californian Mama died of a heart attack in 1974 at the age of 32?

 Sport & Leisure — At which golf course is the US Masters held each year?

 Science & Tech — What is a celestial visible light spectrum better known as?

 True or False? — Henry Ford established the first automobile production line; true or false?

ANSWERS: PAGE 280

Food & Drink
Where would you find a spirit safe?

Natural World
What famous 19th-century ornithologist published the elaborately illustrated *The Birds Of America*?

History
What war did the Light Brigade charge in?

Culture & Belief
What is the correct formal way to address an archbishop?

Stage & Screen
What was the connection between Darth Vader and the Green Cross Code Man?

Written Word
What school bully did George Macdonald Fraser make the hero of a series of humorous novels?

Music
When would you hear an intermezzo?

Famous People
8th December 1980 was the day the music died for fans of what artist?

Sport & Leisure
Which two sports comprise the biathlon?

Science & Tech
What two colours lie at the opposite ends of the rainbow?

True or False?
It is possible to get to the end of a rainbow; true or false?

ANSWERS: PAGE 280

Food & Drink — What is Mulligatawny?

 Natural World — What group of individuals swear their ethical fitness in the Hippocratic Oath?

 History — What street did the Great Fire of London start in?

 Culture & Belief — Before 1752, on what date did the year begin in Britain?

 Stage & Screen — What three films have each won 11 Oscars?

 Written Word — What was the name of Don Quixote's sidekick?

 Music — What are 'whiskers on kittens, bright copper kettles and warm woollen mittens'?

 Famous People — Rockers Richie Sambora and Tommy Lee have both married which beautiful blonde?

 Sport & Leisure — How many times did Jackie Stewart win the Formula One World Drivers' Championship?

 Science & Tech — What does the Mohs scale measure?

 True or False? — Humans have more body hairs than apes; true or false?

ANSWERS: PAGE 281

Food & Drink
What country does chop suey come from?

 Natural World
Air is mostly composed of which two gases?

 History
Which organisation was the predecessor of the United Nations?

 Culture & Belief
Which is known as the senior service?

 Stage & Screen
What two actors played the part of Vito Corleone in *The Godfather* series?

 Written Word
What name was given to the survey of England ordered by William the Conqueror in 1086?

 Music
Who sang *(If Paradise Is) Half As Nice*?

 Famous People
What animator was responsible for *The Seventh Voyage of Sinbad and One Million Years BC*?

 Sport & Leisure
What sport's English governing body had W. G. Grace as its first president?

 Science & Tech
What disorder was called French Disease by the English, and English Disease by the French?

 True or False?
The tune of *God Save The Queen* is known in over 20 countries worldwide to different words; true or false?

ANSWERS: PAGE 281

Food &
Drink

What product was originally marketed as 'Liquid Beef'?

Natural
World

Where is Queen Maud Land?

History

Who was Eisenhower's vice-President?

Culture &
Belief

Who was the royal subject of a famous painting by Hans Holbein?

Stage &
Screen

What director, famed for his westerns, has won more Oscars than any other?

Written
Word

Whose masterpiece was the *Divina Commedia* (or *Divine Comedy*)?

Music

What did Molly Malone die of?

Famous
People

Help, The Three Musketeers and two of the four *Superman* films were the work of what US director?

Sport &
Leisure

Who won the first University Boat Race between Oxford and Cambridge?

Science
& Tech

What is said to have given Newton his first clue about the existence of gravity?

True or
False?

The surface coating for non-stick pans was invented by a Mr Teflon; true or false?

ANSWERS: PAGE 282

Food & Drink

What food did the Aztecs use as currency?

Natural World

What was the first antibiotic?

History

What American became president of Ireland?

Culture & Belief

In the language of flowers, what is represented by a red rose?

Stage & Screen

What Stanley Kubrick film did he himself ban from British cinemas?

Written Word

Who wrote *A Clockwork Orange*?

Music

What does the musical term 'fortissimo' mean?

Famous People

The Magic Roundabout was created by the father of what Oscar-winning British actress?

Sport & Leisure

Which boxing heavyweights have held both the Olympic and professional titles?

Science & Tech

What does the computing acronym 'WYSIWYG' mean?

True or False?

St Vitus is the patron saint of dancers; true or false?

ANSWERS: PAGE 282

Food & Drink
What were commuters urged to go to work on in the 1960s?

 Natural World
What are aphids more commonly known as?

 History
What Irishman became president of Israel?

 Culture & Belief
How many labours had Hercules to perform to win his freedom?

 Stage & Screen
Who is the only person called Oscar ever to have won an Oscar?

 Written Word
In what special restaurant would you find Max Quordlepleen?

 Music
What pub on the city road does the singer visit in *Pop Goes The Weasel*?

 Famous People
What heart-throb was known as The King of Hollywood?

 Sport & Leisure
How long does the famous Le Mans sports-car race last?

 Science & Tech
How many constellations are there?

 True or False?
New York was originally called Jorvik after it was founded by the Viking Leif Ericsson; true or false?

ANSWERS: PAGE 283

Food & Drink
What shape is farfalle pasta?

Natural World
What is the most northerly county in Ireland?

History
Who called England 'A nation of shopkeepers'?

Culture & Belief
What was the ship in which Jason and his followers set sail to find the Golden Fleece?

Stage & Screen
What film depicted an RAF pilot suspended between a technicolour Earth and monochrome after-life?

Written Word
Whose birthday is celebrated throughout the world on 25th January?

Music
Who said 'follow the van and don't dilly-dally on the way'?

Famous People
Whose catch-phrase was 'Just Like That'?

Sport & Leisure
How many squares are there on a chessboard?

Science & Tech
Where is the smallest muscle in the human body?

True or False?
Pearls come in black, blue and green colours as well as white; true or false?

ANSWERS: PAGE 283

Food & Drink
What does the term 'Napoleon Brandy' signify?

 Natural World
What natural structure in central Australia is known by Aborigines as 'Uluru'?

 History
Who was described as George Bush's best insurance against impeachment?

 Culture & Belief
Name four of the seven virtues.

 Stage & Screen
What Italian director made two films with *Once Upon A Time* in the titles?

 Written Word
Who cut off Samson's hair?

 Music
When is an opera a Grand Opera?

 Famous People
What American president's father co-owned a movie studio?

 Sport & Leisure
Nordic and Alpine are the two main categories of which sport?

 Science & Tech
Which are older, veteran or vintage cars?

 True or False?
The collective term for a group of apes is a 'parliament'; true or false?

ANSWERS: PAGE 284

Food & Drink

What day do Americans traditionally eat turkey?

Natural World

What two things do bees collect?

History

How long, to the nearest 10 years, did the Hundred Years War last?

Culture & Belief

Name five of the seven deadly sins.

Stage & Screen

What classic western was based on a story called *The Tin Badge*?

Written Word

What was done to Count Dracula to make doubly sure he was dead?

Music

What type of music would you expect to hear at the Grand Ole Opry?

Famous People

Who replaced Glen Matlock on bass guitar in The Sex Pistols?

Sport & Leisure

Which two teams contested the first cricket test match?

Science & Tech

What is the only substance capable of cutting a diamond?

True or False?

The British Constitution is stored in the library of the Houses of Parliament; true or false?

ANSWERS: PAGE 284

Food & Drink
What drink did the British in India take as an anti-malarial?

 Natural World
What bird has the largest wingspan?

 History
What famous World War One field marshal drowned off the north of Scotland in 1915?

 Culture & Belief
How long does Passover last?

 Stage & Screen
What unlikely POW movie featured Max von Sydow, Bobby Moore, Sylvester Stallone and John Wark?

 Written Word
What story was inspired by the sinking of the whisky-laden *SS Politician* in 1941?

 Music
Who had a UK top 10 hit in 1967 with a version of *Eidelweiss*?

 Famous People
Whose mammoth movie career ended in a sex-and murder scandal in 1921?

 Sport & Leisure
Who was the last winner of BBC TV's *Pot Black* snooker championship in 1986?

 Science & Tech
What is a polygraph used to detect?

 True or False?
Louis Braille, inventor of readable type for the blind, was not blind himself; true or false?

ANSWERS: PAGE 285

Food & Drink
What is the difference between whisky and whiskey?

 Natural World
What is the fastest bird in the world?

 History
What war was income tax first introduced to finance?

 Culture & Belief
What Christian feast is celebrated on Whit Sunday?

 Stage & Screen
In what film would you find Sean Thornton, Mary Kate Danaher and Michaeleen Oge Flynn?

 Written Word
What two books did Robert Louis Stevenson's hero David Balfour appear in?

 Music
According to the song, what will we do 'though cowards flinch and traitors sneer'?

 Famous People
What music producer was famous for his 'wall of sound' production techniques?

 Sport & Leisure
Who was the first cricketer officially to be recorded hitting a six off each ball in a six-ball over?

 Science & Tech
How many carats are there in pure gold?

 True or False?
Vulcanised rubber was invented by a Mr Pirelli; true or false?

ANSWERS: PAGE 285

Food & Drink
How many pints of beer are in a hogshead?

 Natural World
What is known as the Staff of Life?

 History
What Englishman was described as 'The Hammer of the Scots'?

 Culture & Belief
How many rooms, to the nearest hundred, are in the world's largest palace in Brunei?

 Stage & Screen
Where in London did the Wombles live?

 Written Word
Sinbad, Aladdin and Ali Baba all originally appeared in what volume?

 Music
What is the libretto of an opera?

 Famous People
Who is singer-songwriter Declan McManus better known as?

 Sport & Leisure
In which Far Eastern country did the martial art of Taekwondo originate?

 Science & Tech
How much would a ten-stone man weigh on Jupiter?

 True or False?
Ernest Hemingway co-wrote the screenplay of the 1946 version of *The Big Sleep*; true or false?

ANSWERS: PAGE 286

Food & Drink
Who invented the breakfast cereal?

 Natural World
What country was also known as the Union of Myanmar?

 History
How many brothers were there in America's Kennedy family?

 Culture & Belief
What country has the dong as its major unit of currency?

 Stage & Screen
What hugely successful film sparked a flood of disaster movies in the 1970s?

 Written Word
What important manuscripts from the time of Jesus were discovered in an Israeli cave 50 years ago?

 Music
What Spanish singing sensation used to play in goals for Real Madrid reserves?

 Famous People
What age was Jesus Christ thought to be when he died?

 Sport & Leisure
What are the two types of canoe used in international racing competitions?

 Science & Tech
Do arteries carry blood to the heart or away from it?

 True or False?
Flames spread more rapidly in a vacuum than in the open air; true or false?

ANSWERS: PAGE 286

Food & Drink
What notorious gambler invented an easy-to-eat snack so he would not have to leave his card table?

 Natural World
What seas are linked by the Kiel Canal?

 History
What was the fate of the Stone of Destiny at Christmas, 1950?

 Culture & Belief
What colour does a Sikh bride wear on her wedding day?

 Stage & Screen
What Hitchcock film shows its action entirely from the viewpoint of a house-bound photographer?

 Written Word
What craft did Madame Defarge perfect in Charles Dickens' *A Tale Of Two Cities*?

 Music
What two singers had hits with *I Will Always Love You*?

 Famous People
Wagner's most famous fan was a politician who often played his music at rallies; who was he?

 Sport & Leisure
What four titles comprise tennis' Grand Slam?

 Science & Tech
Where would you expect to find a convection current?

 True or False?
Ho Chi Minh was told that he could become the world's greatest pastry chef if he gave up politics; true or false?

ANSWERS: PAGE 287

Food & Drink
What kind of fish is a kipper?

Natural World
What is unusual about the Manx cat?

History
Who beat whom in the Six Day War?

Culture & Belief
What did the Romans call Manchester?

Stage & Screen
What Christmas classic assured cinemagoers that 'Every time a bell rings, an angel gets its wings'?

Written Word
Who was Thornfield Hall's mad inhabitant in *Jane Eyre*?

Music
What dance craze was originally devised to promote the song *Achy Breaky Heart*?

Famous People
What ballerina was *The Dying Swan* ballet specially written for?

Sport & Leisure
Which country has dominated world-class chess?

Science & Tech
What was the first hormone to be identified?

True or False?
Skin is the largest body organ; true or false?

ANSWERS: PAGE 287

Food & Drink
What are the eggs of the sturgeon better known as?

 Natural World
Where would you find the Forbidden City?

 History
What French Protestant changed his religion to become king declaring 'Paris is worth a Mass'?

 Culture & Belief
Under the new Pinyin language system for English speakers of Chinese, what is Peking known as?

 Stage & Screen
What future film director shot to fame as the darkhaired one in TV's *Starsky and Hutch*?

 Written Word
Who did Sherlock Holmes rent his Baker Street rooms from?

 Music
Who had a hit in the US and Britain with *Achy Breaky Heart*?

 Famous People
Who was the last-surviving member of Hollywood's hard-living Rat Pack?

 Sport & Leisure
Which country first put up the yachting trophy, the America's Cup?

 Science & Tech
Where could you find The Microscope, The Clock and The Table?

 True or False?
A tympanum is a percussion instrument; true or false?

ANSWERS: PAGE 288

Food & Drink
Who said 'I do not like broccoli ... I am president of the United States and I am not going to eat any more'?

Natural World
In what modern-day country did the city of Troy lie?

History
When, to the nearest 10 years, was the last time you could hire a climbing boy to clean your chimney?

Culture & Belief
What is the world's most-spoken language?

Stage & Screen
What film's publicity read 'Part man. Part machine. All cop'?

Written Word
What book do Rat, Mole, Badger and Toad appear in?

Music
What did William Blake want to build in England's green and pleasant land?

Famous People
What king was called Old Rowley, after a famous stud stallion?

Sport & Leisure
When was the first one-day international cricket match contested?

Science & Tech
What would you expect to find in a body cavity?

True or False?
Sculptures of Christ's crucifixion are known as calvaries; true or false?

ANSWERS: PAGE 288

Food & Drink
What do the German Purity Laws of Reinheitsgebot regulate?

Natural World
How many millions of years have humans been on the Earth, to the nearest million?

History
Who in 1966 were declared to be more popular than Jesus Christ?

Culture & Belief
Calculate: the Plagues of Egypt plus Horsemen of the Apocalypse minus Tribes of Israel; how many are left?

Stage & Screen
What actor played *The Wild One*?

Written Word
Who fell asleep in the Catskill Mountains for 20 years?

Music
What is the highest-pitched woodwind instrument?

Famous People
What traditionally male occupation did Grace O'Malley, Mary Read and Ann Bonny excel at?

Sport & Leisure
What are the colours of the five rings on the Olympic symbol?

Science & Tech
What is light amplification by stimulated emission of radiation better known as?

True or False?
The Hebrew alphabet has 44 letters; true or false?

ANSWERS: PAGE 289

Food & Drink

Where would you find a parson's nose?

Natural World

In genetics, what do an x chromosome plus a y chromosome add up to?

History

In what century did the potato arrive in Britain?

Culture & Belief

What is the collective term for a group of judges?

Stage & Screen

Three generations of the same family have all been Oscar winners; who are they?

Written Word

Who said in his autobiography, *Goodbye To All That*?

Music

Who wrote *Mad Dogs and Englishmen (Go Out In The Midday Sun)*?

Famous People

How many Rolling Stones have there been?

Sport & Leisure

What teams contested the first-recorded intercounty cricket match in 1709?

Science & Tech

What is the name of the imaginary lines which encircle the Earth parallel to the Equator?

True or False?

Appendicitis is very rare in Africa and Asia; true or false?

ANSWERS: PAGE 289

Food & Drink
What fruit is used to make calvados?

 Natural World
What city was known as Edo before assuming its current name in 1868?

 History
What was destroyed in Paris on 14th July 1789?

 Culture & Belief
Who was Judas Iscariot's replacement?

 Stage & Screen
What sitcom featured Frankie Howerd as a crafty Roman slave?

 Written Word
In what Ian Fleming novel did James Bond make his first appearance?

 Music
What rockabilly rebel recorded the album *Copperhead Road*?

 Famous People
Mr Nelson and Ms Ciccone are rock stars better known by their first names; what are they?

 Sport & Leisure
Which English football team has the largest pitch?

 Science & Tech
Who was the first person to be killed by a train?

 True or False?
Of the 626 people featured on the Bayeux Tapestry, none are women; true or false?

ANSWERS: PAGE 290

Food & Drink
What beer refreshed the parts other beers couldn't reach?

 Natural World
What is the largest city in Europe?

 History
Where was China's 1989 pro-democracy movement crushed by government troops?

 Culture & Belief
What, according to Karl Marx, was the opium of the people?

 Stage & Screen
What 1980s TV character's catch-phrase was 'Gissa job. I can do that'?

 Written Word
Where could you hear the slogan 'All animals are equal but some animals are more equal than others'?

 Music
In what operetta would you hear *He Is An Englishman*?

 Famous People
What rock star's nickname is The Boss?

 Sport & Leisure
What was unique about the White Heather Cricket Club founded at Nun Appleton in Yorkshire in 1887?

 Science & Tech
What is the next number in the sequence: 2, 3, 5, 7, 11 ... ?

 True or False?
Barbers derive their name from the Berber peoples of North Africa; true or false?

ANSWERS: PAGE 290

Food & Drink
What did Adolf Hitler ban on the day he proclaimed the Third Reich?

 Natural World
What substance are lignite and anthracite forms of?

 History
When, to the nearest 10 years, was the Louvre first opened to the public?

 Culture & Belief
What is the most commonly used word in written English?

 Stage & Screen
Who was the animator in *Monty Python's Flying Circus*?

 Written Word
Who wrote *The Great Gatsby*?

 Music
What song did Donny Osmond and Tab Hunter have in common?

 Famous People
What famous child star later became US representative to the UN and ambassador to Ghana?

 Sport & Leisure
Who scored England's goals in the 1966 World Cup Final?

 Science & Tech
What was the first planet to be discovered by use of a telescope?

 True or False?
A camel's hump is where it stores water; true or false?

ANSWERS: PAGE 291

Food & Drink
What is the traditional fare on Shrove Tuesday?

 Natural World
What is the lowest area on the Earth's surface?

 History
In what century were the first Olympic Games held in Greece?

 Culture & Belief
What is the term for a painting done on a freshly plastered wall?

 Stage & Screen
What does a best boy do on a film crew?

 Written Word
Whose ghost haunted *Macbeth*?

 Music
What US presidential candidate used Fleetwood Mac's *Don't Stop* as his campaign theme?

 Famous People
By what title is the Earl of Inverness and Baron Killyleagh better known?

 Sport & Leisure
What sport began in Holland, was later popularised in Scotland then dominated by Canada in modern times?

 Science & Tech
What might you see if refraction occurred during precipitation?

 True or False?
An 'oxbow' is the name of a type of knot; true or false?

ANSWERS: PAGE 291

Food & Drink

What raising agent is used in soda bread?

Natural World

Meteorologically, what are the Doldrums?

History

Which British monarch was crowned 11 years after he first became king?

Culture & Belief

What is ironstone?

Stage & Screen

What film was summarised by a critic as 'A building catches fire, some people die, some people don't'?

Written Word

Who was King Arthur's wife?

Music

What popular early-20th-century Irish-American singer was given a papal peerage?

Famous People

What successful American portrait painter was also known for his dots and dashes?

Sport & Leisure

Who was the first British footballer to be knighted?

Science & Tech

In what century was the first city sewer built?

True or False?

Piltdown Man was an archaeologically important pre-historic skull found in Sussex in 1912; true or false?

ANSWERS: PAGE 292

Food & Drink
What region of France does claret come from?

 Natural World
What is Europe's highest mountain?

 History
Why did American drinkers cry into their beer in January 1920?

 Culture & Belief
What would you be doing if you were performing an arabesque?

 Stage & Screen
What was the name of the bespectacled, intelligent, plain girl in *Scooby Doo*?

 Written Word
What was the first land Gulliver visited on his travels?

 Music
Who wrote *Mack The Knife*?

 Famous People
Who has been the only divorced president of the US?

 Sport & Leisure
When was the first Tour de France held?

 Science & Tech
How many spokes has a snowflake?

 True or False?
A panda is a member of the bear family; true or false?

ANSWERS: PAGE 292

Food & Drink 'Christmas is coming and ...' what are getting fat?

 Natural World What deadly disease was finally declared eradicated in 1980?

 History What other two countries joined the Common Market at the same time as the UK?

 Culture & Belief When do Spanish children receive their Christmas presents?

 Stage & Screen What Oscar-winning animator helped create Bugs Bunny, Daffy Duck and the Road Runner?

 Written Word What George Bernard Shaw play was the inspiration for the musical *My Fair Lady*?

 Music Who went to number 1 in the UK chart in 1972 with *Son Of My Father*?

 Famous People What nationality was T. S. Eliot?

 Sport & Leisure How many hoops are used in a game of croquet?

 Science & Tech What is the smallest constellation?

 True or False? If Force is measured in Newtons, the force of an apple dropping to the ground is roughly 1 Newton; true or false?

ANSWERS: PAGE 293

Food & Drink
What puts the fizz in fizzy drinks?

 Natural World
What trip did the book *The Worst Journey In The World* relate?

 History
Why were London's journalists flushed with relief on 2nd February 1852?

 Culture & Belief
What name are members of the Society of Jesus better known by?

 Stage & Screen
What is the connection between Broccoli and James Bond?

 Written Word
Who was Tom Sawyer's best friend?

 Music
What military campaign did Tchaikovsky's *1812 Overture* celebrate?

 Famous People
What colony, later to become a country, did Cecil Rhodes found?

 Sport & Leisure
What was given to the British Open golf champion before the claret-jug trophy was introduced in 1872?

 Science & Tech
In what decade was the first photograph taken?

 True or False?
The word 'dunce' began as a term of abuse among followers of quarrelling medieval philosophers; true or false?

ANSWERS: PAGE 293

Food & Drink
What colour would you turn food if you added beta carotene to it?

Natural World
What is a death cap?

History
What faith was Henry VIII called the Defender of?

Culture & Belief
What peoples prefer to be known as Kooris?

Stage & Screen
What film KO'd the competition for Best Film Oscar in 1976?

Written Word
Who is the main character in the poem with the line 'Rats! They fought the dogs and killed the cats'?

Music
Who wrote and first performed the R & B classic *Johnny B. Goode*?

Famous People
Who said in 1982 'Mount Everest is now littered with junk from bottom to top'?

Sport & Leisure
What is the longest race in the world?

Science & Tech
How did the QWERTY keyboard get its name?

True or False?
Casanova was expelled from a seminary for alleged homosexuality; true or false?

ANSWERS: PAGE 294

Food & Drink
What beans are cooked to give baked beans?

Natural World
What animal was the first to be domesticated systematically?

History
What colour is the ribbon of the Victoria Cross?

Culture & Belief
What is the Pentateuch?

Stage & Screen
What de Gaulle lookalike was the star of *Jour de Fête* and *Monsieur Hulot's Holiday*?

Written Word
What king's three daughters were Goneril, Regan and Cordelia?

Music
What musical monarch was said to have penned the tune *Greensleeves*?

Famous People
Who is unique in modern Europe as the only man to have founded his own church and political party?

Sport & Leisure
The Grand National, the Laurels and the Scurry Gold Cup are all classic races for what animals?

Science & Tech
Where would you find the Sea of Tranquillity?

True or False?
Vladimir Heavy Draught is a Russian beer; true or false?

ANSWERS: PAGE 294

What is arrowroot most commonly used for?

What is Britain's only poisonous snake?

What Conservative said 'We must build a kind of United States of Europe'?

Roman, Gothic, Ogee and Horseshoe are all types of what?

What was Frederico Fellini's 1959 vision of the sweet life in Rome?

What book, written in the 1920s, was the subject of an obscenity trial when finally published in 1960?

What rock legend was the subject of Don McLean's *American Pie*?

Who once ferried people across Niagara Falls on a high-wire wheelbarrow?

What does 'karate' mean?

What planet's orbit takes it nearest to Earth?

Spiders do not belong to the insect world; true or false?

ANSWERS: PAGE 295

Food & Drink

What is sucrose more commonly known as?

 Natural World

What species outnumber all others on Earth put together?

 History

Who described life in the Royal Navy as 'rum sodomy and the lash'?

 Culture & Belief

What was unusual about the Gorgons' hairstyles?

 Stage & Screen

What Japanese film classic was *The Magnificent Seven* based on?

 Written Word

Who wrote *The Ballad Of The Sad Café*?

 Music

What fairy tale did the original Engelbert Humperdinck set to music?

 Famous People

What poet and diabolist claimed to be the Beast from the Book of Revelation?

 Sport & Leisure

In what four disciplines do women gymnasts compete in competition?

 Science & Tech

What is toxicology the study of?

True or False?

The flags of Poland and Indonesia are identical; true or false?

ANSWERS: PAGE 295

Food & Drink What additive is thought to cause Chinese Restaurant Syndrome?

 Natural World What century did the common dodo become extinct in?

 History Which commoner received a state funeral in 1965?

 Culture & Belief What 1955 design in glass by Raymond Loewy is now a classic?

 Stage & Screen What Ingmar Bergman film sees a knight playing chess with Death to prolong his own life?

 Written Word What novel won the Booker Prize for Salman Rushdie?

 Music Who scored a two-time hit with his *Shotgun Wedding*?

 Famous People Whose nickname was The Welsh Wizard?

 Sport & Leisure Which country is the home of hurling?

 Science & Tech Which has the shorter wavelength – light waves or radio waves?

 True or False? No mammal can fly (except in an aeroplane); true or false?

ANSWERS: PAGE 296

Food & Drink — Why is royal jelly so called?

 Natural World — How much blood is in the average human adult body?

 History — What US president was said not to be able to fart and chew gum at the same time?

 Culture & Belief — What is the highest rank in the Royal Navy?

 Stage & Screen — Who did Robert de Niro portray in his Oscar winning performance in *Raging Bull*?

 Written Word — What poet drowned in the Mediterranean near Viareggio in August 1822?

 Music — Who did Cab Calloway call 'a low-down hoochie-coocher'?

 Famous People — Who was Greek artist Domenikos Theotokopoulos better known as?

 Sport & Leisure — India and Pakistan between them won the gold medal in what sport at every Olympics from 1928 to 1968?

 Science & Tech — What was the Earth's first artificial satellite?

 True or False? — Guests at the world's only underwater hotel in Florida have to scuba-dive to their rooms; true or false?

ANSWERS: PAGE 296

Food & Drink
What drink is made from molasses?

Natural World
Where is the Great Barrier Reef?

History
What was the official title of the Poll Tax?

Culture & Belief
What design style did the 1925 Exposition des Arts Décoratifs in Paris give rise to?

Stage & Screen
Who promised 'I'll be back'?

Written Word
Who was the deformed sexton in Victor Hugo's *Notre Dame De Paris*?

Music
Who wrote *The Mighty Quinn*?

Famous People
Who was the last Hanoverian monarch of Britain?

Sport & Leisure
Greco-Roman and Freestyle are the two main types of which sport?

Science & Tech
What is a CAT scanner generally used to find?

True or False?
Buffalo Bill once kicked off a football match at Glasgow's Hampden Park; true or false?

ANSWERS: PAGE 297

Food & Drink
What are prunes before they are dried?

Natural World
What makes a humming bird hum?

History
How many Cinque Ports were there?

Culture & Belief
What 1931 design by Henry C. Beck unravelled a maze for Londoners?

Stage & Screen
What words appear on the scroll beneath the MGM lion?

Written Word
What newspaper did Clark Kent write for?

Music
What famous song is set to the music of Elgar's *Pomp and Circumstance March No. 1*?

Famous People
Who did Mark Antony appoint king of the Jews?

Sport & Leisure
The Edmonton Oilers, the Chicago Black Hawks and the Toronto Maple Leafs compete in what sport?

Science & Tech
What satellite passed Jupiter in 1979, Saturn in 1981, Uranus in 1986 and Neptune in 1989?

True or False?
Over 350 separate languages have been officially recorded in the tiny kingdom of Tonga; true or false?

ANSWERS: PAGE 297

Food & Drink

What pudding was named after an Australian opera singer?

Natural World

What islands did Darwin visit to get evidence in support of his theories of natural selection?

History

Who did Margaret Thatcher feel she could do business with in 1984?

Culture & Belief

What country used *The Internationale* as its national anthem until 1944?

Stage & Screen

Who played The Artful Dodger in the 1968 film musical *Oliver!*?

Written Word

What writer of the macabre penned *The Fall Of The House Of Usher* and *The Masque Of The Red Death*?

Music

What campaigning singer-songwriter wrote and performed *Cats In The Cradle*?

Famous People

What famous jazz singer was known as 'Lady Day'?

Sport & Leisure

Which was the first European team to win football's World Cup?

Science & Tech

What is measured by an anemometer?

True or False?

Guy Fawkes was trying to blow up the House of Commons; true or false?

ANSWERS: PAGE 298

Food & Drink
What did Jesus do at the Cana wedding feast?

 Natural World
How many chromosomes are in a normal human body cell?

 History
What Prime Minister gave Britain the three-day week?

 Culture & Belief
What do American babies wear on their bottoms?

 Stage & Screen
Name two of the three films which have won Oscars for animator Nick Parks.

 Written Word
What was the name of Bertie Wooster's club?

 Music
Who, according to Robert Burns' song, did the deil, or devil, dance away with?

 Famous People
What small item is Alec Issigonis famous for designing?

 Sport & Leisure
How many players does a Gaelic Football team have?

 Science & Tech
What recurrent stellar visitor to Earth was featured on the Bayeux Tapestry?

 True or False?
The Morris Mini was the first British car to sell one million; true or false?

Food & Drink

What red meat has the lowest fat content?

Natural World

What animal's name means 'river horse'?

History

What was the relationship between Indian prime ministers Jawaharlal Nehru and Indira Gandhi?

Culture & Belief

Where can the Wallace Monument be found?

Stage & Screen

Who played Dr Kildare in the long-running 1960s TV series?

Written Word

What million-selling book caused Alexander Solzhenitsyn's deportation from the USSR in 1973?

Music

What Viennese father and son were renowned masters of the waltz?

Famous People

What did the 'F' in JFK stand for?

Sport & Leisure

What is the highest possible judo grade?

Science & Tech

What man-made vehicle holds the all-time speed record?

True or False?

Nitrogen is the second-biggest component of the air we breathe; true or false?

ANSWERS: PAGE 299

Food & Drink
How many people did Jesus feed with five loaves and two fish?

 Natural World
How long, to the nearest metre, is the adult human small intestine?

 History
What president called his country 'a rainbow nation at peace with itself and the world'?

 Culture & Belief
What notorious Mormon church leader was a polygamist with reputedly over 50 wives?

 Stage & Screen
What musical featured the songs *Surrey With The Fringe On Top* and *Oh What A Beautiful Morning*?

 Written Word
Who wrote *Brighton Rock*?

 Music
What musician and producer did Cait O'Riordan leave the Pogues to marry?

 Famous People
What two famous Irishmen were involved in the biggest sex scandals of the Victorian era in Britain?

 Sport & Leisure
In what sport would you find a foil and an épée?

 Science & Tech
What is the common name of iron pyrites?

 True or False?
A constellation called Norma can be seen from the Southern Hemisphere; true or false?

ANSWERS: PAGE 299

Food & Drink
What cake is traditionally eaten on Easter Sunday?

 Natural World
What unit of measurement was King Henry I's arm used to define?

 History
Which university is older – Oxford or Cambridge?

 Culture & Belief
How many pints of beer would you expect from a flagon?

 Stage & Screen
What political group featured in Leni Riefenstahl's film *Triumph Of The Will*?

 Written Word
What was William Wordsworth describing when he wrote 'Earth hath not anything to show more fair'?

 Music
What big-band leader popularised 'swing' in 1935?

 Famous People
Whose nickname was The Desert Fox?

 Sport & Leisure
What is the racquet used in lacrosse called?

 Science & Tech
If a submarine submerged to 10 fathoms, how far below the surface would it be?

 True or False?
Croissants were first made by French bakers to celebrate a victory in battle over the Turks; true or false?

ANSWERS: PAGE 300

Food & Drink

What are Java, Columbian and Kenyan?

Natural World

If diamond is the hardest mineral, what is the softest?

History

Who offered a New Deal to the American nation during the Depression?

Culture & Belief

Which part of a ship is the Union Jack flown from – front or back?

Stage & Screen

What cult American TV show was always introduced by its creator, Rod Serling?

Written Word

Name the Three Musketeers.

Music

What, according to Brendan Behan, 'went jingle-jangle all along the banks of the Royal Canal'?

Famous People

Who announced his retirement by saying that he wanted to get out with his greatness intact?

Sport & Leisure

What newspaper originally sponsored the Tour of Britain Milk Race for cyclists?

Science & Tech

What substance causes plants to be green?

True or False?

A booklouse is someone who reads books excessively; true or false?

ANSWERS: PAGE 300

Food & Drink
Which contains more caffeine - coffee beans or tea leaves?

 Natural World
What period of Earth's history came first - Jurassic or Carboniferous?

 History
What are the Tower of London's Yeomen of the Guard better known as?

 Culture & Belief
What was St Paul's trade?

 Stage & Screen
What *Dallas* regular first made his name playing opposite a genie in *I Dream of Jeannie*?

 Written Word
How did James Joyce immortalise 16th June 1904, the day he first 'walked out' with his future wife, Nora?

 Music
What song originally by Lord Rockingham's XI, was used in a wine-gums commercial in the mid 1990s?

 Famous People
Who is fourth in line to the British throne?

 Sport & Leisure
Who is the most-capped Scottish footballer?

 Science & Tech
What Apollo space mission put the first men on the Moon?

 True or False?
Sir Walter Raleigh invented an early form of the bicycle; true or false?

ANSWERS: PAGE 301

Food & Drink
What would you be eating if you had a toad in the hole?

 Natural World
At what angle does the Earth tilt towards the Sun?

 History
What did Melbourne, Derby and Aberdeen have in common?

 Culture & Belief
What is the oldest cathedral in Britain?

 Stage & Screen
What was the name of the Ewings' ranch in *Dallas*?

 Written Word
What was the name of Bill Sikes' dog in *Oliver Twist*?

 Music
What American DJ first coined the term 'rock-and roll music'?

 Famous People
What princess won a gold disc for a duet with Bing Crosby?

 Sport & Leisure
Besides lawn tennis, what sport has its English headquarters at Wimbledon?

 Science & Tech
What is trinitrotoluene better known as?

 True or False?
Margaret Thatcher's tenure of office was the longest of any woman prime minister; true or false?

ANSWERS: PAGE 301

Food & Drink
What fruit was traditionally eaten on Mothering Sunday and Palm Sunday?

 Natural World
What is the speed of sound at ground level?

 History
What king was encouraged by a spider's perseverance to try and try again?

 Culture & Belief
Who was the American continent named after?

 Stage & Screen
What island was the home of detective Jim Bergerac?

 Written Word
What two travellers went *Around The World In Eighty Days*?

 Music
According to the carol, of all the trees that are in the wood, which one bears the crown?

 Famous People
What was the connection between Chang and Eng?

 Sport & Leisure
How many players are there in a water polo team?

 Science & Tech
What is the process used to split atomic particles and create massive energy release?

 True or False?
Rock Around The Clock was the first single to sell more than one million copies; true or false?

ANSWERS: PAGE 302

Food & Drink
What make up the three layers in Millionaire's Shortcake?

 Natural World
What part of Oliver Cromwell's body was found at his post-mortem to be almost twice the normal size?

 History
What did Hannibal cross the Alps for?

 Culture & Belief
Which country has more schools than any other?

 Stage & Screen
Who was *To The Manor Born*?

 Written Word
What bear of very little brain lived in the Hundred Acre Wood?

 Music
What Barry McGuire tune topped the chart for the protest movement in 1965?

 Famous People
What teen idol shot to fame in 1970 with the Partridge Family?

 Sport & Leisure
What game was originally known as 'kitten ball'?

 Science & Tech
Copper, zinc and what other metal make up German silver?

 True or False?
Tony Blackburn presented the first edition of *Top Of The Pops*; true or false?

ANSWERS: PAGE 302

Food & Drink
What are hash browns?

 Natural World
Who swore before the Inquisition that the Earth revolved around the Sun?

 History
What renowned sailor and explorer lies in a watery grave off Panama?

 Culture & Belief
If a Welshman added pump and pum cant together, what would be the total?

 Stage & Screen
What holiday camp catch-phrase was the title of an 1980s sitcom?

 Written Word
According to Oscar Wilde, what type of man knows the price of everything and the value of nothing?

 Music
Whose persona was Ziggy Stardust?

 Famous People
Who led the Prague Spring in 1968?

 Sport & Leisure
Which three sports feature in the triathlon?

 Science & Tech
What was it that drove hatters mad?

 True or False?
The soft drink Kia-Ora takes its name from the Maori word for 'good health'; true or false?

ANSWERS: PAGE 303

Food & Drink How much is in a punnet?

Natural World What makes the Bolivian city of La Paz virtually fireproof?

History What aquatic event took place off Griffin's Wharf in Boston Harbour, 1773?

Culture & Belief What city is called after the Greek goddess Athene?

Stage & Screen Who played the voice of the baby in *Look Who's Talking*?

Written Word Who was Lady Chatterley's Lover?

Music Who declared *Je Ne Regrette Rien*?

Famous People Who was Second World War radio announcer William Joyce better known as?

Sport & Leisure What was the first north European team to win football's European Cup?

Science & Tech What is an imaginary number?

True or False? The bowie knife was invented by the famous American frontiersman Jim Bowie; true or false?

ANSWERS: PAGE 303

Food & Drink
What fruit is used to flavour Aurum liqueur?

 Natural World
What does a hippophile have a particular interest in?

 History
What year did the *Mayflower* arrive in America?

 Culture & Belief
What is the English translation of the French word 'cocorico'?

 Stage & Screen
Who took the title role in *I, Claudius*?

Written Word
What grew in the garden of *Mary, Mary, Quite Contrary*?

Music
What group's name was inspired by Keith Moon's verdict that they would go down like a lead balloon?

Famous People
Who was the last viceroy of India?

Sport & Leisure
Where is elephant soccer played?

Science & Tech
What name is given to a person whose body lacks melanin?

True or False?
The Isle of Man was the first place to give women the vote; true or false?

ANSWERS: PAGE 304

Food & Drink
What is frangipane?

 Natural World
What nature-loving saint is the patron of ecologists?

 History
Who led the Free French government in exile during the Second World War?

 Culture & Belief
How many letters are used in the world's shortest alphabet, on the Solomon Islands?

 Stage & Screen
What soap is set around events on Ramsay Street?

 Written Word
Who was the bemused, planet-hopping hero of *The Hitch-Hiker's Guide To The Galaxy*?

 Music
Who was called the Queen of Soul?

 Famous People
By what name is the 15th-century Balkan leader Vlad the Impaler immortalised in literature?

 Sport & Leisure
Where is the World Professional Snooker Championship played?

 Science & Tech
What did alchemists strive to do?

 True or False?
John F. Kennedy was the youngest-ever US president; true or false?

ANSWERS: PAGE 304

Food & Drink
Where did chocolate originate?

Natural World
What mythical undersea land was known as the lost continent?

History
What prime minister did Winston Churchill describe as 'a modest man with much to be modest about'?

Culture & Belief
Who did J. B. S. Haldane call 'the greatest Jew since Jesus'?

Stage & Screen
What do *The Young Ones*, *The Thin Blue Line* and *Blackadder* all have in common?

Written Word
What medieval Italian civil servant made his own name a by-word for cynicism with his book, *The Prince*?

Music
What group of supposed brothers was at the forefront of punk with *Sheena Is A Punk Rocker!*?

Famous People
1978 was the year of the Three Popes – who were they?

Sport & Leisure
Which English Premiership team began life as Dial Square FC?

Science & Tech
Along with protons and electrons, what other particle goes to make up atoms?

True or False?
Blood group O negative is the commonest blood type in the UK; true or false?

ANSWERS: PAGE 305

Food & Drink
Which are generally hotter – green or red chillis?

Natural World
What function does the human appendix perform?

History
What political party introduced the old-age pension?

Culture & Belief
Who dreamt of a ladder, changed his name and fathered 12 children to lead Israel's 12 tribes?

Stage & Screen
What 1970s US drama featured a family living through the Depression in Virginia's Blue Ridge Mountains?

Written Word
What did the famous Sun headline 'Gotcha' refer to?

Music
According to the song, what did I spy on the streets of Laredo?

Famous People
What politician's criticisms were likened to being savaged by a dead sheep?

Sport & Leisure
In what sport is the Camanachd Cup the premier competition?

Science & Tech
If oxygen is O^2, what is O^3?

True or False?
Queen Victoria was the first European monarch to use a telephone; true or false?

ANSWERS: PAGE 305

Food & Drink
What is haslet?

Natural World
Name two of the four creatures that the Bible says were sent to plague the Egyptians.

History
Why did the prime minister and cabinet end up under the table in 10 Downing Street on 7th February 1991?

Culture & Belief
What do bungalows, pundits and verandahs all have in common?

Stage & Screen
What famous film director makes a cameo appearance at the end of *The Blues Brothers*?

Written Word
What famous children's tale features a Canadian orphan called Anne Shirley?

Music
At what event were all the ants fancy-dancing with the fleas?

Famous People
Who said 'A man in the house is worth two in the street'?

Sport & Leisure
How many countries did the 1996 Tour de France pass through?

Science & Tech
How many bytes are there in a kilobyte of computer memory?

True or False?
William Caxton invented the printing press; true or false?

ANSWERS: PAGE 306

Food & Drink
What did the Aztecs cut off what they called the testicle tree?

 Natural World
What did Peter hear after he had disowned Jesus three times?

 History
When, to within five years, were driving tests introduced in Britain?

 Culture & Belief
What would an Irishman do with a boreen?

 Stage & Screen
What is a clapper board used for?

 Written Word
What document was described as 'the longest suicide note in history'?

 Music
What rock-and-roll quartet was the first white act to play Harlem's Apollo Theatre?

 Famous People
What Nazi war criminal sentenced at Nuremberg served the longest sentence?

 Sport & Leisure
What was the UEFA Cup originally known as?

 Science & Tech
What common ailment can be cured by acetylsalicylic acid?

 True or False?
The first vacuum cleaner was so large that it was horse-drawn and could not get inside houses; true or false?

ANSWERS: PAGE 306

Food & Drink What did Oliver Twist ask for more of?

 Natural World What is the southernmost point in the British Isles?

 History How did John Hinckley try to impress Jodie Foster in 1981 ?

 Culture & Belief If livestock is a farmer's animals, what is dead stock?

 Stage & Screen What is the name of Postman Pat's black-and-white cat?

 Written Word What poet was described as 'Mad, bad, and dangerous to know'?

 Music Who is the more famous brother of Mike McGear of The Scaffold?

 Famous People Irishman Arthur Wellesley gave his name to what type of footwear?

 Sport & Leisure What colour is Mayfair on a Monopoly board?

 Science & Tech What organ in the body produces insulin?

 True or False? Chinese typewriter keyboards have around 1500 characters; true or false?

ANSWERS: PAGE 307

Food & Drink
What spirit is made from potatoes?

 Natural World
What is the biggest lake in Britain?

 History
Who were Churchill's Few?

 Culture & Belief
What Chinese philosopher was so revered he was worshipped as a god?

 Stage & Screen
Which famous 1960s pop star provided the TV voice of *Thomas the Tank Engine*?

 Written Word
Who wrote *The First Blast Of The Trumpet Against The Monstrous Regiment Of Women*?

 Music
Where was the Tamla Motown record company first established?

 Famous People
Why did Rolls-Royce change their car's badge colour from red to black?

 Sport & Leisure
What tournament was thought up in 1955 by Gabriel Hanot, soccer editor of French newspaper *L'Equipe*?

 Science & Tech
What road-safety device was invented by Percy Shaw in 1934?

 True or False?
The Caesarean section operation was named after Julius Caesar who was thought to have been born that way; true or false?

ANSWERS: PAGE 307

Food & Drink
What vegetable are G.I.s credited with introducing to Britain?

Natural World
What is normally the longest-lived animal?

History
In what year did the Bank of England replace pound notes with coins?

Culture & Belief
What is the British name of the organisation known as Little Bees in Switzerland and Ladybirds in Italy?

Stage & Screen
Who was the proprietor of *Fawlty Towers*?

Written Word
Who wrote *One Hundred Years Of Solitude*?

Music
What is the name Motown short for?

Famous People
Who was the first music star to be screamed at by young fans?

Sport & Leisure
What are the colours of the three jerseys awarded during the Tour de France?

Science & Tech
Cheriton in Britain and Sargette in France have a common link – what is it?

True or False?
As well as cuckoo birds, cuckoo bees also exist; true or false?

ANSWERS: PAGE 308

Food & Drink
What vegetable did Mark Twain describe as 'Cabbage with a college education'?

Natural World
What mammal has webbed feet, a duck-like bill and lays eggs?

History
Who said, 'A week is a long time in politics'?

Culture & Belief
What island was King Arthur taken to after being wounded in his final battle?

Stage & Screen
Who was the guiding hand behind Kermit the Frog and Miss Piggy?

Written Word
Who was *Down And Out In Paris And London*?

Music
Who composed the music for such blockbusters as *Star Wars*, *Superman* and *Raiders Of The Lost Ark*?

Famous People
What famous singer starred in the world's first talkie?

Sport & Leisure
What do cyclists feel when they hit the 'bonk'?

Science & Tech
What freezes to form 'dry ice'?

True or False?
The socialist republicans were the rebels in the Spanish Civil War; true or false?

ANSWERS: PAGE 308

Food & Drink
What are Ben and Jerry known for?

Natural World
What birds eat, sleep and breed on the wing?

History
What event does the children's rhyme *Ring-A-Ring O' Roses* commemorate?

Culture & Belief
Who was the Apostle of the Gentiles?

Stage & Screen
What cult US TV show launched the careers of Steve Martin, Bill Murray, John Belushi and Dan Aykroyd?

Written Word
Who did Sherlock Holmes describe as 'The Napoleon of Crime'?

Music
What instrument did Glenn Miller play?

Famous People
Whose nickname was 'The Little Tramp'?

Sport & Leisure
What are the discs used in tiddlywinks called?

Science & Tech
What is a computer's footprint?

True or False?
Stonefish is the name of a type of coral; true or false?

ANSWERS: PAGE 309

Food & Drink — What is glorious about August 12th?

 Natural World — How many capitals does South Africa have?

 History — In what country did the sauna originate?

 Culture & Belief — What three saints' crosses are represented on the Union Flag?

 Stage & Screen — What were the names of the Flowerpot Men?

 Written Word — Where did Professor Moriarty meet his death at the hands of Sherlock Holmes?

 Music — What member of *Monty Python's Flying Circus* provided the theme song for *One Foot In The Grave*?

 Famous People — Who led the famous Dambusters raid during the Second World War?

 Sport & Leisure — What Scottish pastime did Hugh Munro give his name to?

 Science & Tech — Where would you find a lancet, a galilee and a finial?

 True or False? — The tibia bone's connected to the radius bone; true or false?

ANSWERS: PAGE 309

Food & Drink — What Italian pudding's name translates as 'Pick-me-up'?

Natural World — In what modern-day country is the ancient city of Petra?

History — What did Vincent van Gogh do after quarreling with Paul Gauguin?

Culture & Belief — What do Hindus and Buddhists call the state of oneness with god?

Stage & Screen — What real-life brothers played the Kray Twins on film?

Written Word — Who ended his nightly diary entries with the words, 'And so to bed'?

Music — Who was George Michael's partner in Wham!?

Famous People — Who was lead singer of the group Nirvana?

Sport & Leisure — Who was the first BBC Sports Personality Of The Year?

Science & Tech — What are Doric, Ionic and Corinthian all types of?

True or False? — Kellogg first developed breakfast cereals in 1906 as a health food for psychiatric patients; true or false?

ANSWERS: PAGE 310

Food & Drink
To what profession of Frenchman would you give a *pourboire* (literally meaning 'for drinking')?

 Natural World
In which Scottish region would you find John O' Groats?

 History
Which country was Montezuma ruler of?

 Culture & Belief
What is Montezuma's Revenge?

 Stage & Screen
Who played *The Blues Brothers*?

 Written Word
Whose political views were set out in the book entitled *My Struggle*?

 Music
Who was *Kissing With Confidence* in 1983?

 Famous People
What famous model of the 1960s was known as The Shrimp?

 Sport & Leisure
Who missed the penalty that put England out of the 1996 European Championships?

 Science & Tech
How many ounces to the pound are there in the troy system?

 True or False?
A carillon is the specific name given to a chorister in Canterbury Cathedral; true or false?

ANSWERS: PAGE 310

Food & Drink
The name of which liqueur literally translates as 'the drink that satisfies'?

Natural World
What country uses a dram as a unit of currency?

History
How many prime ministers, including Tony Blair, have there been in the present queen's reign?

Culture & Belief
What would be your special subject if you studied apiology?

Stage & Screen
Which Tellytubby carries a red handbag?

Written Word
What was the name of the bowler-hatted, sober-suited brothers in *Tin Tin*?

Music
At first sight, what was unusual about the 1980s pop group The Thompson Twins?

Famous People
During the BSE scare, what government minister made his daughter eat burgers for a photo-call?

Sport & Leisure
What modern-day pub game was originally introduced into America by the Pilgrim Fathers?

Science & Tech
Which children's toy was invented in 1900 by Frank Hornby?

True or False?
Germany's Oktoberfest beer festival always begins in September; true or false?

ANSWERS: PAGE 311

Food & Drink
What country holds the record for largest consumption of alcoholic spirits?

 Natural World
What creature comprises the largest part of a mole's diet?

 History
What does the Woolsack symbolise?

 Culture & Belief
Who sits on the Woolsack in the House of Lords?

 Stage & Screen
What is the name of the green Tellytubby?

 Written Word
Whose dog was Snowy?

 Music
What two colours featured in a 1955 hit for Eddie Calvert?

 Famous People
Mel Blanc, the voice of Bugs Bunny, was allergic to what?

 Sport & Leisure
On a Monopoly board, what colour is Old Kent Road?

 Science & Tech
In a British electric plug, what colour is the live wire?

True or False?
Eating carrots helps you see in the dark; true or false?

ANSWERS: PAGE 311

Food & Drink How much sugar does the average Briton eat every month?

 Natural World Canterbury Cathedral is in which county?

 History What modern European capital was established by the Moors in the 10th century as Medina Majerit?

 Culture & Belief Which city's art gallery is the Prado?

 Stage & Screen What comedy-drama programme features a dog called Diefenbacker?

 Written Word According to T. S. Eliot, what is April?

 Music What was the nickname of R&B musician Antoine Domino?

 Famous People Where was Archbishop Thomas Beckett murdered in the 12th century?

 Sport & Leisure How many pieces in a domino set have a six on them?

 Science & Tech Which pin on a three pin plug is the longest?

 True or False? Writer Arthur Conan Doyle created the first fictional detective; true or false?

ANSWERS: PAGE 312

Food & Drink
How many lumps of sugar are in a can of non-diet fizzy drink?

Natural World
Which sex of elephants have tusks – male or female?

History
What addition was once made to army uniforms to stop soldiers wiping their noses on their sleeves?

Culture & Belief
Which church's great bell is the largest in the UK?

Stage & Screen
How much were actress Betty Grable's renowned 'million dollar legs' actually insured for?

Written Word
Which Victorian detective described his toughest cases as 'three-pipe problems'?

Music
Which of the three Bee Gees was the youngest?

Famous People
Louis Farrakhan is a leader of which organisation?

Sport & Leisure
Which animal appears on the badges of both Dumbarton FC and Coventry FC?

Science & Tech
What are the three primary colours for artists?

True or False?
Legendary sleuth Sherlock Holmes played the saxophone; true or false?

ANSWERS: PAGE 312

Food & Drink — What is the main ingredient of patatas bravas?

 Natural World — What is known as the lungs of New York City?

 History — What job did Joseph Goebbels do in Adolph Hitler's Nazi government?

 Culture & Belief — What hand does the Statue of Liberty hold her torch in?

 Stage & Screen — Name the five members of the Simpsons family.

 Written Word — Why did Mae West advise you should keep a diary?

 Music — What 1970 tune was the original theme music for *Top Of The Pops*?

 Famous People — Who was the first king of a unified Italy?

 Sport & Leisure — What is the height of a badminton net?

 Science & Tech — How many colours are generated by a colour TV tube?

 True or False? — The three primary colours are red, green and blue; true or false?

ANSWERS: PAGE 313

Food & Drink

What is tofu made of?

Natural World

One of the two ancient granite obelisks called Cleopatra's Needles is in London; where is the other?

History

Who did the original Peeping Tom peep at in 1040?

Culture & Belief

The Statue of Liberty holds a torch in one hand; what is in the other?

Stage & Screen

Who is the sidekick of Mr Burns, head of Springfield's nuclear plant, in *The Simpsons*?

Written Word

What boffin's equation A=X+Y+Z gave A as success, X as work, Y play, and Z keeping your mouth shut?

Music

Who first had a hit with *Whole Lotta Love*?

Famous People

Lady Godiva rode naked through Coventry in which century?

Sport & Leisure

In what field competition are the winners those who move backwards most effectively?

Science & Tech

What is the Statue of Liberty made of?

True or False?

Adolf Hitler took his pet rat, Otto, with him everywhere he went; true or false?

ANSWERS: PAGE 313

Food & Drink
Which vegetable is the basis of quorn?

Natural World
How much skin, to the nearest two square feet, does an average-sized man have?

History
How many of his wives did Henry VIII divorce?

Culture & Belief
Which three of the seven virtues are regarded as being the most important?

Stage & Screen
What brunette starred alongside Marilyn Monroe in the film *Gentlemen Prefer Blondes*?

Written Word
According to Anita Loos, who do gentlemen marry?

Music
'Paul' is Paul McCartney's second name; what is his first?

Famous People
How old was Marilyn Monroe when she died?

Sport & Leisure
How many gold medals did the UK win in the 1996 Olympic Games?

Science & Tech
What was the name of the world's first clone of an adult animal?

True or False?
The Beatles were the first British group to have a number 1 hit in the USA; true or false?

ANSWERS: PAGE 314

Food & Drink

What did Shirley Conran say life is too short to do?

Natural World

How many pairs of ribs do humans have?

History

Three of Henry VIII's six wives shared a name; what was it?

Culture & Belief

In the Book of Genesis, where did the Land of Nod lie?

Stage & Screen

Name two of the three women who originally appeared in the 1970s TV series, *Charlie's Angels*.

Written Word

What sibling asked 'Am I my brother's keeper?'

Music

What famous Beatles song was supposedly based on a fantastical painting by John Lennon's son Julian?

Famous People

What famous musician owned a film company called Handmade Films?

Sport & Leisure

Where were the 1944 Olympic Games supposed to be held?

Science & Tech

What mathematical sign is used to describe the ratio of a circle's circumference to its diameter?

True or False?

Vera Lynn was the first British female singer to have a number 1 hit in the USA; true or false?

ANSWERS: PAGE 314

Food & Drink
What is the source of the red food colouring cochineal?

Natural World
What insect's bite can spread malaria?

History
How many of Henry VIII's wives outlived him?

Culture & Belief
How many months are there in the Hindu calendar?

Stage & Screen
What were Ned, Min and Bluebottle better known as?

Written Word
What demonic name means 'Lord of the Flies'?

Music
What group cancelled their 1998 UK tour because of their projected tax bill?

Famous People
Who sailed yachts called *Gipsy Moth*?

Sport & Leisure
What was so unusual about Abebe Bikila's winning run in the 1960 Olympic Marathon?

Science & Tech
What number is pi (π) usually given?

True or False?
In 1995–6, the Beatles earned more money than the Rolling Stones; true or false?

ANSWERS: PAGE 315

Food & Drink
A cake baked at 350°F would need what number on a gas cooker?

Natural World
Which chromosome from its father determines whether a baby will be a girl, X or Y?

History
How was Henry VIII of England related to James IV of Scotland?

Culture & Belief
Who was the Norse god of Thunder?

Stage & Screen
In the *Star Wars* movies, what was Darth Vader's name before he went to the Dark Side of the Force?

Written Word
What film was based on the story *Do Androids Dream of Electric Sheep*?

Music
Who recorded a record-breaking album called *Songs for Swingin' Lovers*?

Famous People
What rival once said of Frank Sinatra 'He had the voice of a lifetime. Unfortunately, it's my lifetime'?

Sport & Leisure
Who was accused of tripping US runner Mary Decker-Slaney in the 1984 Olympic 5000m race?

Science & Tech
Who invented the centigrade thermometer?

True or False?
The Volkswagen Beetle was designed by a Herr Porsche; true or false?

ANSWERS: PAGE 315

Food & Drink What substance in tea is a passion killer?

 Natural World How many pairs of chromosomes does a human cell contain?

 History In Shakespeare's play, Hamlet stabs Polonius through the arras; what is an arras?

 Culture & Belief What do the initials T&GWU stand for?

 Stage & Screen What county is the long-running BBC radio series *The Archers* set in?

 Written Word What is the most filmed Shakespeare play?

 Music What is the connection between the bands Bananarama and Shakespear's Sister?

 Famous People Who won an Oscar for his role as Private Angelo Maggio in the 1953 film *From Here to Eternity*?

 Sport & Leisure Which former cricketer walked in Hannibal's footsteps for charity?

 Science & Tech Where was the ill-fated cruise ship *Titanic* built?

 True or False? Hamlet has the most lines of all Shakespeare's characters; true or false?

ANSWERS: PAGE 316

Food & Drink
What is the English term for the dish the Italians call *Zuppa Inglese*?

 Natural World
In what modern-day country is the ancient city of Carthage?

 History
What is the only instance of the George Cross ever having been awarded to an entire population?

 Culture & Belief
What is the second-highest British gallantry award?

 Stage & Screen
Who played Sam Spade in *The Maltese Falcon*?

 Written Word
What kind of animal was Beatrix Potter's Mrs Tiggywinkle?

 Music
In the song, what do The Crystal Chandeliers light up?

 Famous People
What youthful film prodigy claimed that he had started at the top and worked down?

 Sport & Leisure
What race commemorates the arrival in ancient Athens of news of a victory over the Persians?

 Science & Tech
Where in Britain is there a miniature copy of the Eiffel Tower?

 True or False?
The Eiffel Tower was designed by a Mr Eiffel; true or false?

ANSWERS: PAGE 316

Food & Drink
What type of dish is bouillabaisse?

Natural World
What part of the eye determines its colour?

History
How many pre-decimal pennies was a florin worth?

Culture & Belief
What, according to the proverb, do listeners never hear?

Stage & Screen
What film features a central scene at the top of the big wheel in a deserted Viennese funfair?

Written Word
In the story *The Three Billy Goats Gruff*, what fearsome creature was hiding under the bridge?

Music
In the song *Jailhouse Rock*, what did the warder tell Sad Sack to use instead of a partner?

Famous People
What publishing tycoon's life was reputedly the inspiration for the film *Citizen Kane*?

Sport & Leisure
How many Formula 1 races had Mika Hakkinen won before the 1998 Grand Prix race season?

Science & Tech
How tall, to the nearest 10 ft, is London's St Paul's Cathedral?

True or False?
Jackie Stewart won more grand prix races than Nigel Mansell; true or false?

ANSWERS: PAGE 317

Food & Drink
What kind of sauce is the basis for tartare sauce?

Natural World
A liger is a cross between which two animals?

History
How many decimal pennies was a florin worth at the time of decimalisation?

Culture & Belief
When poverty comes in at the door, what does the proverb say flies out of the window?

Stage & Screen
Who was Diana Rigg's predecessor as John Steed's sidekick in *The Avengers*?

Written Word
What is the name of the little boy in the *Winnie-the-Pooh* stories?

Music
What band was Louise a member of before leaving to go solo?

Famous People
Who was noted for his stylised illustrations for Oscar Wilde's *Salome*?

Sport & Leisure
Who were the second Scottish football team to win nine successive league championships?

Science & Tech
What type of bridge construction is the Forth Rail Bridge?

True or False?
The MGM lion is named Leo; true or false?

ANSWERS: PAGE 317

Food & Drink
What drink should be colourless, odourless and tasteless?

Natural World
What is the least amount of rain likely to fall on Brazil's rainforest in a year (to the nearest 10 in)?

History
How many military Crusades were fought to take the Holy Land between 1096 and 1204?

Culture & Belief
In the zodiac, what are the three water signs?

Stage & Screen
Who runs the Post Office in Postman Pat's village, Greendale?

Written Word
What aquatic-sounding Chinese novel and TV series tells of Robin Hood-type bandits fighting corruption?

Music
What did my true love send to me on the seventh day of Christmas?

Famous People
The Lake District town of Grasmere was home to what well-loved poet?

Sport & Leisure
Which swimming event was introduced to the Olympics in LA in 1984?

Science & Tech
What is an Archimedes screw used to lift?

True or False?
French Perrier Water was originally produced by an Englishman; true or false?

ANSWERS: PAGE 318

Food & Drink — What type of pastry is used to make Mille Feuille?

Natural World — What is the crane fly more commonly known as?

History — What foreign-born monarch began the building of the Tower of London?

Culture & Belief — Who was the Roman goddess of the hearth?

Stage & Screen — What actor writes and plays TV's Alan Partridge?

Written Word — What poet's love was like a red, red rose?

Music — What song has the lines 'He rattled his marracas close to me, In no time I was trembling at the knees'?

Famous People — How many times was Charles de Gaulle president of France – two, three or four?

Sport & Leisure — Where were the Commonwealth Games held in 2002?

Science & Tech — What building in London is set at exactly 0 degrees longitude?

True or False? — On the London Underground every year, more single gloves are lost than pairs of gloves; true or false?

ANSWERS: PAGE 318

Food & Drink

What does Mille Feuille mean?

Natural World

To the nearest thousand miles, how far is Peking from Buenos Aires?

History

Who recognised 'the wind of change' blowing through Africa?

Culture & Belief

According to Arthurian legend, who, as well as Arthur, loved Guinevere?

Stage & Screen

Who produced the classic Western *The Wild Bunch*?

Written Word

What did Neil Kinnock say was the most important book in the Tory education system?

Music

Three of the members of Abba were called Agnetha, Bjorn and Benny; who was the fourth?

Famous People

What was the previous job of former TV presenter Robert Kilroy-Silk?

Sport & Leisure

What game would you be playing if you played spoilfive?

Science & Tech

Who is the British physicist noted for his investigation of black holes?

True or False?

The pigtail was banned in China in the early 20th century; true or false?

ANSWERS: PAGE 319

Food & Drink
What robust cheese might you be served alongside port?

Natural World
What is the famous English village set entirely in a prehistoric stone circle?

History
What was the name of Butch Cassidy and the Sundance Kid's gang?

Culture & Belief
What is the largest sculpture in Britain?

Stage & Screen
What classic film was the 1970s TV series *Alias Smith and Jones* based on?

Written Word
Why did Jane Eyre not marry Mr Rochester at the first attempt?

Music
What stirring anthem originally went under the less-than-snappy title *War Song for the Rhine Army*?

Famous People
What opera singer was romantically involved for years with Artistotle Onassis?

Sport & Leisure
Who won the Tour de France in 1998?

Science & Tech
Bibendum is the French name for which trademark creature?

True or False?
The word guillotine came from an amalgamation of the French words for 'neck' and 'sever'; true or false?

ANSWERS: PAGE 319

Food & Drink
What turns the blue veins in cheese blue?

 Natural World
What two countries share the West Indian island of Hispaniola?

 History
What country did dictators Papa Doc and Baby Duvalier rule for almost 30 years?

 Culture & Belief
What traditionally is thanks given for at Thanksgiving Day in the US?

 Stage & Screen
Name one of the two adult dalmatians in *101 Dalmatians*.

 Written Word
If a play is described as Shavian, what does this tell you about it?

 Music
What is Irish singer-songwriter George Ivan better known as?

 Famous People
What 20th-century wit was said to have declared 'Television is for appearing on, not looking at'?

 Sport & Leisure
What four tournaments comprise golf's Grand Slam?

 Science & Tech
Diesel for farm machinery is taxed differently from DERV. How can you tell them apart?

 True or False?
The Channel Tunnel is the world's longest underwater tunnel; true or false?

ANSWERS: PAGE 320

Food & Drink
If you ordered pastrami on rye, what would you be served?

Natural World
Where is the ocean of storms?

History
What country's flag reached the moon first?

Culture & Belief
Who was the founder of the Sikh religion?

Stage & Screen
What is the name of Mickey Mouse's dog?

Written Word
In *1984* by George Orwell, who is the dictator of Oceania?

Music
Which Dean Martin hit starts 'When the moon hits your eye like a big pizza pie'?

Famous People
Name one of the two late 'spaced-out' celebrities who took part in the first-ever space burial in 1997.

Sport & Leisure
How many times has Seve Ballesteros won the British Open golf tournament?

Science & Tech
How many planets are in our solar system?

True or False?
Joan Collins once appeared as the captain's love interest in *Star Trek – The Next Generation*; true or false?

ANSWERS: PAGE 320

Food & Drink
What colour are pistachio nuts?

 Natural World
What group of islands does Fair Isle belong to?

 History
What well-loved British institution clocked up its half-century in 1998?

 Culture & Belief
What event are hot cross buns supposed to commemorate?

 Stage & Screen
Who played the part of Fagin in the 1968 film *Oliver!*?

 Written Word
What legendary film reviewer said *'Frankenstein* and *My Fair Lady* are really the same story'?

 Music
Who is Paul McCartney's musician brother?

 Famous People
Who was the Queen's unexpected companion in her bedchamber in July 1982?

 Sport & Leisure
Ice hockey is the national sport of what country?

 Science & Tech
Which textile is only genuine if handwoven in the Outer Hebrides?

 True or False?
The Shetland pony is the smallest breed of horse; true or false?

ANSWERS: PAGE 321

Food & Drink
Which ingredient in some toothpastes is also used to make scones rise?

Natural World
How many teeth does an adult human have?

History
What was special about the sailing of the ship *Empire Windrush* to Britain in 1948?

Culture & Belief
What festival is celebrated three days after Maundy Thursday?

Stage & Screen
What type of product was featured on the first TV commercial?

Written Word
What pirate had a parrot that cried 'Pieces of eight! Pieces of eight!'?

Music
What wacky 1960s band featured both Mike McGear and poet Roger McGough?

Famous People
Which Pacific island eventually became home to Scottish author Robert Louis Stevenson?

Sport & Leisure
When was the Wimbledon Tennis Championship opened to professionals?

Science & Tech
How many funnels did the *Titanic* have?

True or False?
If your diet consisted only of rabbit meat, you would die of vitamin deficiency; true or false?

ANSWERS: PAGE 321

Food & Drink
The MAFF regulates food labelling. What does MAFF stand for?

 Natural World
What is the only country in the world where half of all citizens are classified as being overweight?

 History
What date is inscribed on the book held by the Statue of Liberty?

 Culture & Belief
If an American told you he had just swallowed a goofball, what would you expect him to do?

 Stage & Screen
What lollipop-sucking cop from the 1970s had the catch-phrase 'Who loves ya, baby'?

 Written Word
In Shakespeare's play, why did Julius Caesar dislike Cassius' appearance?

 Music
Name two of the three members of the enduringly influential 1960s band Cream.

 Famous People
What name was super-slim model and actress Lesley Hornby better known by?

 Sport & Leisure
What is the maximum weight of a flyweight boxer?

 Science & Tech
How many sides has a trapezium?

 True or False?
The USA consumes more sweets annually per head of population than Denmark; true or false?

ANSWERS: PAGE 322

Food & Drink
Gunpowder can be what kind of drink?

Natural World
What American state is Montpelier the capital of?

History
What is the significance of the date 1776 inscribed on the Statue of Liberty's book?

Culture & Belief
What nationality was the Good Samaritan of the Bible story?

Stage & Screen
What two TV series did the characters Bob Ferris and Terry Collier appear in?

Written Word
What was the name of Long John Silver's parrot?

Music
What was the record chosen in 1973 to launch Richard Branson's new Virgin label?

Famous People
What did the navigator Amerigo Vespucci give his name to?

Sport & Leisure
How often is yachting's America's Cup held?

Science & Tech
What country had the better-quality high-definition TV first – USA or UK?

True or False?
All the tea in China is less than all the tea in India; true or false?

ANSWERS: PAGE 322

Food & Drink What type of fruit is ananas another name for?

Natural World What is the non-technical name for the sternum?

History What early American president is pictured on the one-dollar bill?

Culture & Belief Which of Hercules' tasks ultimately caused his death?

Stage & Screen What famous British cartoonist drew the characters in Disney's animated feature film *Hercules?*

Written Word What was the name of Noddy's house?

Music What two brothers formed the backbone of the 1960s group The Kinks?

Famous People What famous artist is married to actress and cake-maker Jane Asher?

Sport & Leisure Who recorded snooker's first official maximum break, in 1955?

Science & Tech How is the clavicle commonly known?

True or False? Per head of population, the UK drinks more tea than Ireland; true or false?

ANSWERS: PAGE 323

Food & Drink
What do vichyssoise and gazpacho have in common?

Natural World
What is the name of the sleep stage when dreaming occurs?

History
What London street was synonymous with fashion in the 1960s?

Culture & Belief
How many years would you be married if you were celebrating your lace anniversary?

Stage & Screen
What Hollywood star first found fame on the classic TV western series *Rawhide*?

Written Word
Which novel begins, 'It was the best of times, it was the worst of times ...' ?

Music
What did Molly Malone cry in the streets of Dublin?

Famous People
Which acclaimed English actor began his TV career on the 1970s children's programme *Playaway*?

Sport & Leisure
What team has won the World Cup more than any other?

Science & Tech
What distinction did Valentina Tereshkova achieve in 1963?

True or False?
One person in every five on Earth is Chinese; true or false?

ANSWERS: PAGE 323

Food & Drink

Which between vodka and red wine will give a worse hangover?

Natural World

What do the initials REM stand for?

History

What was unusual about 19th-century British prime minister Spencer Percival?

Culture & Belief

With which religion would you associate the Lotus Scripture?

Stage & Screen

What TV character's catch-phrase was 'Drink! Feck! Arse! Girls!'?

Written Word

What foot did Dubliner Christy Brown kick with in the book and double-Oscar-winning 1989 film?

Music

Who took the hit song *Things Can Only Get Better* as their theme song in 1997?

Famous People

Which one of his senior Labour Party colleagues did Denis Healey liken to a garden gnome?

Sport & Leisure

How many countries have won the World Cup?

Science & Tech

How many units of alcohol are there in a 70cl bottle of 40% proof whisky?

True or False?

Neil Armstrong first stepped onto the moon with his right foot; true or false?

ANSWERS: PAGE 324

Food & Drink
Which spirit is made by distilling wine?

Natural World
What distinguishes marsupials from other mammals?

History
What town was obliterated by an eruption of Vesuvius in 79 AD?

Culture & Belief
What would be the interest of someone interested in hostelaphily?

Stage & Screen
What TV programme does Assistant Director Walter Skinner appear in?

Written Word
What is the name of the garage-owner in the Noddy stories?

Music
What did Paul Simon say we could call him in his 1986 top ten hit?

Famous People
Film directors Fellini, Bogdanovich, Godard and Huston all shared the same original job; what was it?

Sport & Leisure
What team was the only one to remain unbeaten in the 1974 World Cup?

Science & Tech
How many units of alcohol is considered a safe weekly limit for women?

True or False?
'X' is the least-used letter in the English Alphabet; true or false?

Food & Drink
What name is commonly given to the indigestible substance also known as cellulose or fibre?

 Natural World
What type of bird do sailors call a gooney bird?

 History
What has been banned from British television since 1 August 1965?

 Culture & Belief
Do British male subjects have to bow to the Queen?

 Stage & Screen
What two of TV's *Friends* characters are brother and sister in the programme?

 Written Word
What does Noddy do for a living?

 Music
How was Peter & Gordon's 1964 US no. 1 *World Without Love* important for Lennon & McCartney?

 Famous People
Which pop group still features in the top twenty highest earning entertainers, over 30 years after splitting up?

 Sport & Leisure
What is a poop deck?

 Science & Tech
Which organ of the body is affected by cirrhosis?

 True or False?
Cigarettes are the most popular duty-free purchase; true or false?

ANSWERS: PAGE 325

Food & Drink
What percentage of the fibre we eat is absorbed by the body?

Natural World
What colour is the gemstone citrine?

History
What made the Sinn Fein MP Constance Markievicz notable in British political history?

Culture & Belief
What would you be afraid of if you suffered from venustaphobia?

Stage & Screen
What kind of girls were Pussy Galore, Mary Goodnight and Kissy Suzuki?

Written Word
In what Ian Fleming novel was Bond's preference for martini 'shaken not stirred' first noted?

Music
Who came from a land down under to have a simultaneous hit in the UK and US in 1982?

Famous People
What quizmaster first played James Bond, in a radio production?

Sport & Leisure
What type of sailing boat is the fastest?

Science & Tech
Au is the symbol of which element?

True or False?
In the Gulf state Qatar, men outnumber women by almost two to one; true or false?

ANSWERS: PAGE 325

Food & Drink
Potatoes contain a significant amount of which vitamin?

 Natural World
How many million years old is the earth thought to be, to the nearest 500?

 History
What period in American history does antebellum refer to?

 Culture & Belief
Name any one of the three creeds declaring the Christian faith.

 Stage & Screen
What children's radio series began with the words 'Are you sitting comfortably? Then I'll begin'?

 Written Word
According to the King James Bible, who was Lucifer?

 Music
Which former Radio 2 DJ had two number 1 hits in the 1950s?

 Famous People
George Washington was the first American president; who was the second?

 Sport & Leisure
Where would you have expected to see athletes Hunter, Wolf and Lightning?

 Science & Tech
How much does a litre of water weigh?

 True or False?
John F. Kennedy was the first Catholic president of the US; true or false?

ANSWERS: PAGE 326

Food & Drink Vitamin D is only found in foods which contain what?

 Natural World What city does the Isis flow through?

 History What was the National Socialist German Workers' Party better known as in the 1930s?

 Culture & Belief The Greek goddess of hunting was called Artemis; what name did the Romans give her?

 Stage & Screen Which Disney character was named after a newly discovered planet in 1930?

 Written Word In what year was the *Highway Code* first published: 1927, 1929 or 1931?

 Music What pop group appeared in the film *The Great Rock & Roll Swindle*?

 Famous People Which Labour Party leader died of a heart attack in 1994?

 Sport & Leisure Name one of the two Thames bridges that the University Boat Race passes under.

 Science & Tech The world's first traffic lights were in London; when did they date from (within five years)?

True or False? There is a city called Rome on every continent; true or false?

ANSWERS: PAGE 326

Food & Drink

What is marmite?

Natural World

What collective noun describes both a group of kangaroos and a group of monkeys?

History

What is the oldest British order of chivalry?

Culture & Belief

What would an Australian do with a billabong – play it, eat it or paddle in it?

Stage & Screen

What is unusual about the films directed by 'Alan Smithee'?

Written Word

What American writer coined the phrase 'the beat generation'?

Music

What did the Jolly Swagman from *Waltzing Matilda* camp in the shade of?

Famous People

Who was the British politician primarily responsible for the abolition of the slave trade?

Sport & Leisure

What was tennis player Evonne Cawley's maiden name?

Science & Tech

What European city was home to the world's first contraceptive clinic in 1881?

True or False?

Spiral staircases in medieval buildings were always built clockwise; true or false?

ANSWERS: PAGE 327

Food & Drink What American town is the home of Coca-Cola?

 Natural World What holiday islands' former name translates as The Fortunate Islands?

 History Which Scottish king killed Duncan and was himself killed by Duncan's son Malcolm?

 Culture & Belief In what country have half a million Christians been killed for their beliefs since 1975?

 Stage & Screen What kind of car was Disney's Love Bug?

 Written Word What, according to Lady Macbeth, would not sweeten her little hand?

 Music Who gave up his seat to the Big Bopper, on the plane that killed him?

 Famous People Nicholas Breakspear is the only Englishman to become what?

 Sport & Leisure In modern fencing, the swords used are the sabre, epeé and which other?

 Science & Tech What planet does the moon Ganymede belong to?

 True or False? Mars Bars were created by a Mr Mars; true or false?

ANSWERS: PAGE 327

Food & Drink
Pepsi is so called because it was said to cure which ailment?

Natural World
What is the more common term for dyspepsia?

History
Which seafaring leader began life right-handed and ended it left-handed?

Culture & Belief
What is the English translation of Descartes' maxim 'Cogito, ergo sum'?

Stage & Screen
What actor said in a film 'A man's gotta do what a man's gotta do'?

Written Word
What were the magic words that opened the doors of the Forty Thieves' treasure cave?

Music
Who said to a royal variety show audience 'Those in the cheap seats clap, the rest rattle your jewellery'?

Famous People
What ageing Lothario did Shirley Maclaine say was age 50 from the neck up and 14 from the waist down?

Sport & Leisure
Why is Bob Charles unique among winners of golf majors?

Science & Tech
How many moons has the planet Saturn – 8, 12, 18 or 25?

True or False?
George Harrison was the youngest of the Beatles; true or false?

Food & Drink
Fred the flour grader is the trademark of which company?

Natural World
What plant is saffron a product of?

History
In 1752 the Julian calendar was replaced by what?

Culture & Belief
What month in our calendar is called after a Roman emperor?

Stage & Screen
What horror classic promised to pay £10,000 to the first cinema-goer who died of fright watching it?

Written Word
What poor woodcutter discovered the magic words to open the treasure cave of the Forty Thieves?

Music
What record did *Pulp Fiction*'s Vincent and Mia dance to in the twist contest at Jackrabbit Slim's?

Famous People
What US actress was made a French Chevalier of Arts in 1995 in recognition of her film work?

Sport & Leisure
What 20th-century golfing genius retired aged 28, having already won the Grand Slam?

Science & Tech
How many degrees from the Greenwich meridian is the international date line?

True or False?
The Hundred Years War did not last a hundred years; true or false?

ANSWERS: PAGE 328

Food & Drink What substance is the basic ingredient of mead?

 Natural World What is the collective name for a group of badgers?

 History Which English king did Robert the Bruce defeat at Bannockburn?

 Culture & Belief What Christian celebration is Advent a time of preparation for?

 Stage & Screen What was Dirty Harry's surname?

 Written Word Who wrote the *Foundation* trilogy of sci-fi novels?

 Music *The Flowers of the Forest* is a lament for the dead of which battle between England and Scotland?

 Famous People What religion is Richard Gere a follower of?

 Sport & Leisure What was the score in the first ever football international, between Scotland and England?

Science & Tech What comet is thought to have been seen as the Star of Bethlehem, foretelling the birth of Christ?

True or False? Music to be played at 'allegro tempo' would be played at a very slow speed; true or false?

Food & Drink

How many fluid ounces are there in a pint?

 Natural World

What is Mount Godwin-Austen in the Himalayas more commonly known as?

 History

Who led the peasants' revolt in the 14th century?

 Culture & Belief

What Old Testament leader was prepared to sacrifice his son to God?

 Stage & Screen

What did the films *The Odd Couple*, *MASH* and *Nine To Five* have in common?

 Written Word

Which Brontë sister wrote *Wuthering Heights*?

 Music

Who wrote the *1812 Overture*?

 Famous People

Which stars took out a high-profile ad in *The Times* to declare their love 2 months before filing for divorce?

 Sport & Leisure

In bowls, how does a crown green differ from a level green?

 Science & Tech

To the nearest five years, how often does Halley's Comet return?

 True or False?

Nancy Astor was the first woman to address the House of Commons; true or false?

ANSWERS: PAGE 329

Food & Drink — What gives pesto sauce its colour?

Natural World — What is the most northerly line of latitude where the sun can be directly overhead?

History — Who was king of England when Wat Tyler led the peasants' revolt?

Culture & Belief — A person born on 2 September would be which zodiac sign?

Stage & Screen — What was the registration number of Lady Penelope's Rolls Royce in *Thunderbirds*?

Written Word — What arts critic adapted his own novel *A Time to Dance* for TV?

Music — What melancholy name did Tchaikovsky give to his sixth and final symphony?

Famous People — Who is the richest businessman in the world?

Sport & Leisure — What type of sportsman would use a grinner, a palomar and a half-blood?

Science & Tech — In computer terminology, what does DOS stand for?

True or False? — Noah's ark came to rest on Mount Sinai; true or false?

ANSWERS: PAGE 330

Food & Drink What is the main ingredient of egg noodles?

 Natural World What kind of creature is a miller's dog?

 History Which real-life killer first came to the big screen in Alfred Hitchcock's 1926 film *The Lodger*?

 Culture & Belief The Four Horsemen of the Apocalypse rode different-coloured horses; who rode the pale horse?

 Stage & Screen What is the connection between Kermit the Frog and *Star Wars* Jedi master Yoda?

 Written Word How did Scarlett O'Hara and Rhett Butler's daughter die?

 Music Which two singers died within weeks of recording TV shows with David Bowie?

 Famous People Who played the part of Muhammad Ali in the bio-pic of his life, *The Greatest*?

 Sport & Leisure Who regained the World Heavyweight Boxing championship twice?

 Science & Tech What nickname was given to Ronald Reagan's Strategic Defence Initiative?

 True or False? Alfred Hitchcock was born in Singapore; true or false?

ANSWERS: PAGE 330

Food & Drink If herbs are the green parts of plants, what are spices?

 Natural World Who was the first recorded man to cross the Antarctic circle?

 History Which country was split by the 38th Parallel?

 Culture & Belief What do British magicians call their professional ruling body?

 Stage & Screen Fleegle, Bingo, Drooper and Snorky were a bunch of hairy TV pop stars collectively known as what?

 Written Word Which TV critic on *The Observer* newspaper wrote the novels *Metroland* and *Flaubert's Parrot*?

 Music What was the name of the Spice Girls' film?

 Famous People Which two Africans were joint winners of the 1993 Nobel Peace Prize?

 Sport & Leisure What two international cricketing sides met for the first time ever in 1877?

 Science & Tech How long in hours will a colour TV run on one unit of electricity?

 True or False? Madonna's real first name is Mary; true or false?

ANSWERS: PAGE 331

Food & Drink

The goddess of the harvest gives her name to which staple food?

Natural World

Captain Cook was murdered in which island group?

History

Shirley Williams and David Owen were two of the SDP gang of four. Who were the other two?

Culture & Belief

The Greek and Roman gods of the sun shared the same name; what was it?

Stage & Screen

What film featured Bill Murray as a weatherman forced to live the same day over and over again?

Written Word

In *Down with Skool*, who describes poetry as 'sissy stuff that rhymes'?

Music

Who asked you to *Sound Your Funky Horn* and *Shake Your Booty*?

Famous People

Which 1990s artist displayed various animals in tanks of formaldehyde?

Sport & Leisure

Irrespective of which country holds them, where are 'the Ashes' on display?

Science & Tech

Who invented the mercury thermometer?

True or False?

The Sun sells more copies each day than all the quality broadsheets combined; true or false?

ANSWERS: PAGE 331

Food & Drink On average, what do we consume two teaspoons of, every day?

Natural World What American state's nickname is The Last Frontier?

History Who was the last Chinese Emperor?

Culture & Belief What German word describes the spirit of the age?

Stage & Screen Who was Edmund Blackadder's sidekick through the ages?

Written Word How many letters are there in the Greek alphabet?

Music Which British actress/comedienne said 'All I want for Christmas is a Beatle'?

Famous People Who was the first Tudor queen of England?

Sport & Leisure What German football hero was nicknamed The Kaiser?

Science & Tech Eiffel Tower designer Gustave Eiffel also designed locks for which canal?

True or False? *The Sun* has the biggest daily circulation of any English-language newspaper in the world; true or false?

ANSWERS: PAGE 332

Food & Drink

What is the trademark of Bacardi?

Natural World

Name three of the original Cinque Ports on England's south coast.

History

Who founded the Suffragettes in 1903?

Culture & Belief

Whose title is Mikado?

Stage & Screen

What famous film series was Gerald Thomas responsible for?

Written Word

Who was chuffed at pulling Annie and Clarabel?

Music

The D'Oyly Carte opera company is most associated with whose light operas?

Famous People

Mrs Bandaranaike, the world's first woman prime minister, was premier of which country?

Sport & Leisure

Hawaiian Sunny Garcia is a leading exponent of which sport?

Science & Tech

What did Karl Benz name after his daughter?

True or False?

Batman appeared on TV before Superman; true or false?

ANSWERS: PAGE 332

Food & Drink
What procedure removes the the threat of brucellosis from milk?

 Natural World
The Appian Way links Rome with which port?

 History
Who was elected president of the Philippines after people power ousted Marcos?

 Culture & Belief
Where would an American put a diaper?

 Stage & Screen
What classic film series featured the characters W. C. Boggs, D. S. Bung and the Khasi of Kalabar?

 Written Word
What island are the *Thomas the Tank Engine* stories set on?

 Music
Who wrote the songs for Beatles take-off band the Rutles?

 Famous People
In 1953, what Nobel Prize did Winston Churchill win?

 Sport & Leisure
The term 'pegging out' has come to mean dying, but means finishing which sport?

 Science & Tech
In 1903 Antoine Becquerel shared the Nobel Prize for Physics with which married couple?

 True or False?
The founder of the Nobel Peace Prize was also the inventor of dynamite; true or false?

ANSWERS: PAGE 333

Food & Drink

What is a prune?

 Natural World

Which famous port is on the Hawaiian island of Oahu?

 History

Which simple box camera was designed for Kodak by Frank Brownell?

 Culture & Belief

If you had a fender-bender in the US, what would have happened?

 Stage & Screen

What 1960s British comedy film was subtitled *The British position in India*?

 Written Word

What one-time silent-film star was the first actor ever to appear on the cover of *Time* magazine?

 Music

What was the Beatles' first film?

 Famous People

Clement Attlee's biography was called *As It Happened*, but whose was called *As It Happens*?

 Sport & Leisure

What sport would you use a malibu board for?

 Science & Tech

Name one of the companies which developed CDs.

True or False?

Brownsville, Texas, is the hottest city in the USA; true or false?

ANSWERS: PAGE 333

Which sugar features the trademark Mr Cube?

 What substance is stored in the gall bladder?

 Who has controlled Gibraltar for the longest period, Britain or Spain?

 How would you be feeling if you were tristful?

 What colour is Po Tellytubby?

 Which writer's books spawned the 'Harry Palmer' films?

 Who was a 1970s chart-topper with *Can the Can*, *48 Crash* and *Devil Gate Drive*?

 Who was the self-styled Chairman of the Board of the Rat Pack?

 Which British skater won an Olympic gold in 1976?

 Which two sugar magnates never met?

 The blackbird is Britain's commonest bird; true or false?

ANSWERS: PAGE 334

Which two fruits are crossed to make Ugli® fruit?

 What is the modern-day name of the sea that pirates used to call the Spanish Main?

 Who was England's last reigning Tudor monarch?

 What is the collective term for a group of leopards?

 Who played Vito Corleone in *The Godfather Part II*?

 What book by Harper Lee, later made into a film, features the character Boo Radley?

 What film was the chart-topping tune *Duelling Banjos* taken from?

 Which two poets' love affair was chronicled in the film *The Barretts of Wimpole Street*?

 Where was the 1970 World Cup played?

 What does EMI stand for?

 India produces more films each year than the USA; true or false?

Food & Drink
What is the literal translation of the German dish sauerkraut?

Natural World
What is the largest mammal in the world?

History
Who was Britain's last reigning Stuart monarch?

Culture & Belief
Which of the 12 Apostles is the patron saint of tax officials?

Stage & Screen
What comedy series' central character is a Seattle-based radio psychiatrist?

Written Word
Shakespeare's Romeo and Juliet became Tony and Maria in what Broadway smash hit musical?

Music
Who wrote the musical *Blood Brothers*?

Famous People
Who was Elizabeth I's mother?

Sport & Leisure
The St Andrew's Club was founded during the reign of which golf-playing queen?

Science & Tech
Who was the first woman to fly the Atlantic?

True or False?
Iceland's President Finnbogadottir, elected in 1980, was the world's first elected female head of state; true or false?

ANSWERS: PAGE 335

Food & Drink
In America a health warning on bottles and cans advises who not to drink alcohol?

 Natural World
Where is the Napa Valley wine-producing area?

 History
What late-19th century craft movement was the designer William Morris particularly associated with?

 Culture & Belief
What is Sianel Pedwar Cymru more commonly known as?

 Stage & Screen
What is Frasier's second name?

 Written Word
In the Mario Puzo novel, what is the name of *The Godfather*?

 Music
What was the name of the only movie the Monkees ever made?

 Famous People
Which of the services did James Stewart and Clark Gable join in the Second World War?

 Sport & Leisure
What 1976 Olympic gymnast was the first ever to achieve a perfect score?

 Science & Tech
What type of doctors specialise in the care of pregnant women and unborn babies?

True or False?
The English are the world's greatest beer consumers; true or false?

ANSWERS: PAGE 335

Food & Drink
If a Scotsman is eating champit neeps, what is on his plate?

Natural World
Salmon fishing and whisky distilling are associated with a particular Scottish river; what is it?

History
What area was brought under British control by the Opium War?

Culture & Belief
What is the newspaper of the Salvation Army?

Stage & Screen
What classic TV series featured two brothers called Little Joe and Hoss?

Written Word
What is the full name of Major Major in *Catch 22*?

Music
Which unlikely duo paired up on the 1980s' hit *Barcelona*?

Famous People
Which pop star took lead roles in *Ned Kelly*, *Performance* and *Freejack*?

Sport & Leisure
What shape is the field where a baseball match is played?

Science & Tech
On the Mohs hardness scale, what is the hardest mineral?

True or False?
Hong Kong has more skyscrapers than New York; true or false?

ANSWERS: PAGE 336

Food & Drink
How many teaspoons of sugar are there in one packet of jelly?

Natural World
What is Holy Island, off England's north-east coast, also known as?

History
Which type of aeroplanes competed for the Schneider Trophy?

Culture & Belief
Where would you expect to see a Mexican Wave?

Stage & Screen
Who spent years fighting the Autons, Silurians, Sea Devils and Drashigs?

Written Word
In what branch of business are Man Booker Prize sponsors The Man Group?

Music
The Rogers and Hammerstein musical *Carousel* was the source of what famous football anthem?

Famous People
Where was Labour leader John Smith buried?

Sport & Leisure
How many men make up a baseball team?

Science & Tech
Which two stations are connected by the Glasgow to London west coast rail line?

True or False?
The most common surname in both Britain and the USA is Smith; true or false?

ANSWERS: PAGE 336

Food & Drink
UHT milk lasts indefinitely if unopened. What does UHT stand for?

 Natural World
Which major mountain system includes the volcano, Cotopaxi?

 History
In what year did Britain have three kings?

 Culture & Belief
What help was Simon of Cyrene supposed to have given Jesus?

 Stage & Screen
How many of the Magnificent Seven are left alive at the end of the film?

 Written Word
In 1516, Sir Thomas More first used which name for an ideal society?

 Music
What hit did Bill Haley change the lyrics of to avoid anything suggestive?

 Famous People
Which sea captain was set adrift by his crew and later became governor of New South Wales?

 Sport & Leisure
What player claimed the hand of God helped him score a goal in the 1986 World Cup?

 Science & Tech
If diamond is rated 10 on the Mohs hardness scale, what is the rating of talc?

 True or False?
Bill Haley and the Comets were the first American group to have a number 1 hit in the UK; true or false?

ANSWERS: PAGE 337

Food & Drink

Vegetarians will not eat cheese containing which animal derivative?

Natural World

How do frogs breathe while underwater?

History

How was Kublai Khan related to Genghis Khan?

Culture & Belief

What is the name for the 14 books of the Bible that appear in Catholic but not in Protestant versions?

Stage & Screen

What long-running kids' TV show began in 1958 fronted by Christopher Trace and Leila Williams?

Written Word

Who wrote *Slaughterhouse 5*?

Music

Rock Around the Clock was a hit after it featured in which film?

Famous People

Which warrior lived longest: Alexander the Great, Genghis Khan or Attila the Hun?

Sport & Leisure

What was unusual about the 1912 Boat Race?

Science & Tech

Where in the US did the Wright brothers make the first controlled flight?

True or False?

Wilbur Wright was the first man to fly in a heavier-than-air aircraft; true or false?

ANSWERS: PAGE 337

Food & Drink If an egg floats on water, is it fresh or stale?

 Natural World Apart from lying down, what can fish not do as they sleep?

 History When was the United Nations charter signed, in San Francisco?

 Culture & Belief What was The Sweeney cockney rhyming slang for?

 Stage & Screen What cult TV detective series saw Bruce Willis first make his name?

 Written Word Where in Aberdeenshire was Robert Louis Stevenson living when he wrote *Treasure Island*?

 Music Who played the role of Jim Morrison in the 1991 film *The Doors*?

 Famous People Which battle was Nelson's last?

 Sport & Leisure What footballing first did Stanley Matthews achieve in 1965?

 Science & Tech What did Charles Lindbergh call his Atlantic-crossing plane?

 True or False? On the *Bounty*, William Bligh actually held the rank of lieutenant; true or false?

ANSWERS: PAGE 338

Food & Drink
What is the best grain for making beer?

Natural World
Which American state is noted for its bluegrass?

History
Who was the first US president to appear on TV?

Culture & Belief
What day every year does New Orleans' famous Mardi Gras festival take place on?

Stage & Screen
What cult 1960s show featured agents of the United Network Command for Law and Enforcement?

Written Word
What character in *Don Quixote* was called Rosinante?

Music
Which is made of wood – glockenspiel or xylophone?

Famous People
Who is the Italian satirist whose plays include *Can't Pay, Won't Pay*?

Sport & Leisure
Who rode Nijinsky to win the Derby in 1970?

Science & Tech
What pain-killer is derived from the bark of the willow tree?

True or False?
In Scrabble, 'Q' is worth 12 points; true or false?

ANSWERS: PAGE 338

Food & Drink What is the French term used for a bundle or bag of herbs?

 Natural World What is the world's most sparsely populated country?

 History What was the name of Britain's first Polaris submarine?

 Culture & Belief Which month starts with All Saints' Day?

 Stage & Screen What do TV shows *The Man From UNCLE*, *Sapphire and Steel* and *The Invisible Man* have in common?

 Written Word Who won Pulitzer Prizes for *Rabbit is Rich* in 1982 and *Rabbit at Rest* in 1991?

 Music What chart-topping music was the theme to the terrifying 1973 film *The Exorcist*?

 Famous People Charles Dodgson, better known as Lewis Carroll, lectured in which subject at Oxford?

 Sport & Leisure In what year was the Grand National declared void?

 Science & Tech What was the frankencycle?

 True or False? Iceland is the country nearest to the North Pole; true or false?

ANSWERS: PAGE 339

Food & Drink
What is the Italian name for corn meal?

Natural World
What is the world's most densely populated country?

History
Which decade saw Switzerland give its women the vote in national elections?

Culture & Belief
In which month is All Souls' Day?

Stage & Screen
What coveted object did Bob Hope describe as 'a bookend with a sneer'?

Written Word
The memorial to Lewis Carroll in Llandudno is a statue of what?

Music
Who co-wrote *Mull of Kintyre* with Paul McCartney but sold his rights after being declared bankrupt?

Famous People
What celebrity father and daughter duo appeared together in the award-winning film *Paper Moon*?

Sport & Leisure
In croquet, if your balls are black and blue, what colour are your opponent's balls?

Science & Tech
What letter lies to the right of Y on a QWERTY keyboard?

True or False?
Agatha Christie is the most-translated author in the world; true or false?

ANSWERS: PAGE 339

Food & Drink
What kind of fruit is a Cox's Orange Pippin?

 Natural World
What American state is Carson City the capital of?

 History
When was the last execution at the Tower of London (to the nearest 10 years)?

 Culture & Belief
The work of art called *La Gioconda* is better known as what?

 Stage & Screen
How many Oscars did *Brief Encounter*, *Rebel Without A Cause* and *Psycho* win between them?

 Written Word
What Michael Ondaatje story won the Booker Prize in 1992 and the best picture Oscar in 1997?

 Music
What adjective is usually used to describe rock 'n' roller Richard Penniman?

 Famous People
Who was the first actor to refuse an Oscar award?

 Sport & Leisure
Which is larger, a croquet lawn or a tennis court?

 Science & Tech
What 1982 film was computer animation first used in?

 True or False?
Humphrey Bogart won only one Oscar; true or false?

ANSWERS: PAGE 340

Food & Drink
Which biscuit is named after an Italian soldier?

 Natural World
What Hebridean island is Fingal's Cave on?

 History
What state saw the last executions for witchcraft in the USA?

 Culture & Belief
What ancient Celtic festival marks the old year's end with a driving away of the spirits of the newly dead?

 Stage & Screen
What instrument does Lisa Simpson play?

 Written Word
Which novelist created the character of lawyer Atticus Finch?

 Music
What band did Frank Sinatra sing with before going solo?

 Famous People
What more light-footed name was Frederick Austerlitz better known as?

 Sport & Leisure
Which two teams have football grounds called the Stadium of Light?

 Science & Tech
Which lightweight metal is made from bauxite?

 True or False?
Sharp-shooter Annie Oakley once shot a cigarette from between the lips of Kaiser Wilhelm; true or false?

ANSWERS: PAGE 340

Food & Drink

What name is given to a pudding with pears, and very thin toast?

Natural World

What colour is amethyst?

History

Where was the investiture of Prince Charles as Prince of Wales?

Culture & Belief

In Greek mythology what did Prometheus steal from Olympus?

Stage & Screen

Welcome to Berlin was the original title of what famous stage show?

Written Word

In Samuel Beckett's most famous play, what are Vladimir and Estragon doing?

Music

Which soul singer fronted a band called Grand Central, with Prince on guitar?

Famous People

What did *The New York Herald* sponsor Henry Stanley's expedition to do in Africa?

Sport & Leisure

Which boxer was known as the Detroit Destroyer?

Science & Tech

Which aid to navigation is called, in full, radio detection and ranging?

True or False?

Gordon Bennett was a real person and was the newspaper proprietor who sent Stanley to Africa to look for Dr Livingstone; true or false?

ANSWERS: PAGE 341

Food & Drink What kind of fruit are Green Williams?

 Natural World What is the longest mountain range on earth?

 History How many presidents has the USA had, including George W. Bush?

 Culture & Belief In the language of flowers, what does rosemary represent?

 Stage & Screen Who originally played Sally Bowles in the 1968 London stage version of *Cabaret*?

 Written Word Edith, Osbert and Sachaverell were members of what literary family?

 Music Which of Holst's *Planet Suite* depicts the bringer of jollity?

 Famous People Which US president took the decision to drop the first atomic bomb?

 Sport & Leisure Which yacht racing cup was originally called the Queen's Cup?

 Science & Tech Which is the Third Rock From The Sun?

 True or False? Bill Clinton is taller than Abraham Lincoln was; true or false?

ANSWERS: PAGE 341

What method of cooking might an American call broiling?

What is the world's biggest country?

Of the 43 presidents of the USA, how many have been Republicans?

Which British coin has a portcullis on the reverse?

What musical starred Richard Gere in its London stage version and John Travolta in its film?

What novel by nine-year-old Daisy Ashford was published with her mis-spellings intact?

Which new wave band featured guitarist Luke Warm, sax player William Mysterious, and singer Fay Fife?

What country was the dancer Dame Ninette de Valois born in?

Name two cities to have hosted more than one Olympic Games.

What is a one thousand millionth of a second called?

Gerald Ford was never elected to the post of either president or vice-president of the US; true or false?

ANSWERS: PAGE 342

Food & Drink

What kind of fruit is an Elegant Lady?

 Natural World

What fruit was the cargo of the *Bounty* when the crew mutinied?

 History

In what year was the Domesday Book compiled?

 Culture & Belief

What is the first commandment?

 Stage & Screen

Anthony Hopkins, Charles Laughton and Lon Chaney all played a love-sick campanologist; who was he?

 Written Word

A map of what island shows Foremast Hill, Spyglass Hill and Mizzenmast Hill?

 Music

What 1970s band dropped Guildford from their original name?

 Famous People

What famous American family was 1960s actor and Rat Pack member Peter Lawford married into?

 Sport & Leisure

How many eyes can be seen on a deck of cards?

 Science & Tech

A year of which planet is equal to 84 earth years?

 True or False?

Ombrophobia is the fear of umbrellas; true or false?

ANSWERS: PAGE 342

Food & Drink
What is a Pink Lady?

Natural World
Which Scottish island is known as 'Scotland in miniature'?

History
In what battle did Henry V defeat the French in 1415?

Culture & Belief
In the song, how many presents were handed over on the 12th day of Christmas?

Stage & Screen
What was the most enduring and coveted creation of MGM art director Cedric Gibbons?

Written Word
The title of the war novel *Fair Stood the Wind for France* originally referred to what medieval battle?

Music
Which rock singer/producer wrote the words for the Lloyd Webber musical *Whistle Down the Wind*?

Famous People
Explorer Henry Stanley fought in the American Civil War. On which side?

Sport & Leisure
What is the penalty if a show jumper falls off their horse?

Science & Tech
What chemical element has the atomic number one?

True or False?
John F. Kennedy features on the back of the US $50 bill; true or false?

ANSWERS: PAGE 343

Food & Drink
Does a cheesecake contain cheese?

Natural World
What is the modern name for Byzantium?

History
Who was the 'noblest Roman' who fell on his sword near Philippi?

Culture & Belief
How many days after St David's day is St Patrick's day?

Stage & Screen
Where does the action in *Zorba the Greek* actually take place?

Written Word
What Irish writer's novel, *Murphy,* did Dylan Thomas describe as 'Sodom and Begorrah'?

Music
Which American composer wrote *Alexander's Rag Time Band* and *Annie Get Your Gun*?

Famous People
What revolutionary's real name was Vladimir Ilyich Ulyanov?

Sport & Leisure
Who were the losing side in the first World Cup final in 1930?

Science & Tech
What unlikely material was the bodywork of the East German Trabant car made from?

True or False?
Chromophobia is the fear of colour; true or false?

ANSWERS: PAGE 343

Food & Drink

What type of food can be classed as beef, cherry or plum?

Natural World

What is the longest river in China?

History

Which British king was known as Farmer George?

Culture & Belief

What year would be written MCMLXXXIV in Roman numerals?

Stage & Screen

In what Lloyd-Webber musical would you find Rum Tum Tigger, Mungojerrie and Asparagus?

Written Word

Which poet laureate wrote about the religious troubles of his teddy bear?

Music

What instrument would you associate with Julian Lloyd Webber?

Famous People

How did Anne Boleyn die?

Sport & Leisure

Which sport was invented in a Massachusetts YMCA?

Science & Tech

Which housewives' convenience product was invented by Earl Tupper?

True or False?

The Statue of Liberty stands on Ellis Island at New York harbour; true or false?

ANSWERS: PAGE 344

Food & Drink
What term describes spooning hot fat over a roast?

 Natural World
Which island was known as Van Diemon's island?

 History
Which two-piece item of clothing is named after an atomic bomb test site?

 Culture & Belief
The Watchtower is the magazine of which religious body?

 Stage & Screen
Who are the only two characters with names in the stage musical *Godspell*?

 Written Word
Who wrote children's poetry in *The Bad Child's Book of Beasts* and *More Beasts for Worse Children*?

 Music
Dvorak's *New World Symphony* became known as the tune from which adverts?

 Famous People
Richard Block and David Quayle founded which DIY chain?

 Sport & Leisure
What is the name of the Chicago basketball team?

 Science & Tech
Which household convenience was invented by Sir John Harrington?

 True or False?
The modern flush toilet was developed by a Mr Crapper; true or false?

ANSWERS: PAGE 344

Food & Drink
On the EC scale for egg sizes 1–7, is 1 the smallest or largest?

Natural World
Which owl is also known as a screech owl?

History
Which ship sank off Cape Race in 1912?

Culture & Belief
What is St Vitus the patron saint of?

Stage & Screen
What valour award does David Jason's fictional detective Frost hold?

Written Word
Which fictional detective stayed in the same street as Holmes and Watson?

Music
What girl's name is the title of Chuck Berry's first hit?

Famous People
How is Prince Philip related to Queen Victoria?

Sport & Leisure
Which Australian won the men's tennis Grand Slam twice in the 1960s?

Science & Tech
Which two planets do not have moons?

True or False?
The USA has a longer frontier than Russia; true or false?

ANSWERS: PAGE 345

Food & Drink
What food might come as a Coburg, Huffkin or Bloomer?

Natural World
Which is the last US state listed alphabetically?

History
How many days was Edward VIII king for?

Culture & Belief
According to the Bible, who shall inherit the earth?

Stage & Screen
What 1998 smash-hit movie was the first successful film spin-off of a current TV series?

Written Word
What nationality is best-selling travel writer Bill Bryson?

Music
Which member of the Beatles was not in the Quarrymen?

Famous People
William Friese-Greene was a pioneer of which popular entertainment?

Sport & Leisure
Who won a record seven gold medals at one Olympic Games in 1972?

Science & Tech
What are the three primary colours which make up television images?

True or False?
New York was named after James, Duke of York, brother of Charles II; true or false?

ANSWERS: PAGE 345

Food & Drink When might you eat a simnel cake?

 Natural World Which rivers run through Dublin and Cardiff?

 History Which was the first industry to be nationalized in post-war Britain?

 Culture & Belief What does the phrase 'fiat lux' mean?

 Stage & Screen Martin Shaw, Ben Kingsley and Joanna Lumley all appeared in what long-running TV series?

 Written Word Which cult Scottish author adds a middle initial 'M' to his name on his science fiction novels?

 Music Which little boy did the Coasters sing about, asking *Why's everybody always pickin' on me?*?

 Famous People Which modern-day politician once famously declared that there was no such thing as society?

 Sport & Leisure What two winter sports make up the biathlon?

 Science & Tech What is hi-fi abbreviated from?

 True or False? Britain's greatest sailor, Admiral Nelson suffered terribly from seasickness; true or false?

ANSWERS: PAGE 346

Food & Drink
How many calories, to the nearest 10, are in a glass of sweet white wine?

Natural World
What term describes a warm spell of weather in late autumn?

History
The Iran-Contra affair provided guns to fight which Nicaraguan regime?

Culture & Belief
Martin Luther nailed his 95 Theses to the Wittenburg church door in which century?

Stage & Screen
Mr Ed talked his way to stardom in the eponymous 1960s TV show. What was unusual about him?

Written Word
What did Oscar Wilde describe as 'the unspeakable in full pursuit of the uneatable'?

Music
Who did Stevie Wonder sing *Happy Birthday* to in his 1982 single?

Famous People
Who was assassinated at Memphis, Tennessee in 1968?

Sport & Leisure
1,000 Guineas; 2,000 Guineas; The Oaks; The Derby. Name the missing classic horse race.

Science & Tech
What unit of engines' power is equal to 745 watts?

True or False?
New York was home to the world's first skyscraper; true or false?

ANSWERS: PAGE 346

Food & Drink
How many minutes of housework are required to burn off the calories in a 25g bag of crisps?

 Natural World
The Menai Bridge links mainland Wales and which island?

 History
The rationing of what ended on 15 March 1949?

 Culture & Belief
How did French economist Proudhon answer his own question 'What is property?'

 Stage & Screen
What US comedy show started the careers of stars like Eddie Murphy and Billy Crystal?

 Written Word
Author John Buchan became Governor-general of what Commonwealth country?

 Music
Who starred as Pink in the film version of *The Wall*?

 Famous People
Newspaper owner and politician Lord Beaverbrook was born in which country?

Sport & Leisure
Who has won the most motor racing World Championships?

Science & Tech
Where in a building would you find headers, stretchers, halfbats and queen closers?

True or False?
A cummerbund is worn around the head; true or false?

ANSWERS: PAGE 347

Food & Drink
Which has most protein per 100g, baked beans, peanuts or cheddar cheese?

 Natural World
Which three US states start with the letter O?

 History
Whose 1950s economic programme was called The Great Leap Forward?

 Culture & Belief
How many different portraits of Queen Elizabeth II have appeared on British coins?

 Stage & Screen
What colourful children's TV classic opens to the tune of *Barnacle Bill*?

 Written Word
Which newspaper did Lord Beaverbrook say he ran for no other purpose than propaganda?

 Music
Which comic actor had top 10 hits with *Hole in the Ground* and *Right Said Fred*?

 Famous People
Who succeeded Khrushchev as First Secretary of the Soviet Communist Party?

 Sport & Leisure
Who did Virginia Wade beat in the 1977 Wimbledon singles final?

 Science & Tech
Igor Sikorsky designed the first successful version of which method of transport?

True or False?
The Union Jack flies at the front of a ship; true or false?

Food & Drink In the names of beers, what do the amounts 60 Shilling, 70 Shilling and 80 Shilling represent?

 Natural World Which channel divides Wales from Ireland?

 History What was the name given to Ronald Reagan's economic policies?

 Culture & Belief In Rome, the goddess of wisdom was Minerva. Who was her Greek counterpart?

 Stage & Screen What was Dr Who's Time And Relative Dimensions In Space machine better known as?

 Written Word What was the first thing Kingsley Amis said he would buy with his Booker Prize?

 Music Whose book was called *The One Who Writes the Words for Elton John*?

 Famous People How did cosmonaut Yuri Gagarin die?

 Sport & Leisure Which sport features the Sugar Bowl, Rose Bowl and Cotton Bowl?

 Science & Tech Where might you normally see the Welsh phrase 'Pleidiol wyf im gwlad'?

 True or False? Israel has the largest Jewish population in the world; true or false?

ANSWERS: PAGE 348

Food & Drink
What pastry is used to make chocolate eclairs?

Natural World
What colour is the flower of a sunflower?

History
How many British monarchs have there been since 1900?

Culture & Belief
What is the name of the small leather boxes worn by Jewish men during worship?

Stage & Screen
Name three of the *Roads* that Bing Crosby and Bob Hope took?

Written Word
Charles Bukovski wrote the screen play for which film starring Faye Dunaway and Mickey Rourke?

Music
Who were the three members of the Jam?

Famous People
Which director supposedly inspired Ed Wood to pursue his film career?

Sport & Leisure
What nationality were motor racing champions Piquet, Senna and Fittipaldi?

Science & Tech
How many sides does a 20p coin have?

True or False?
The lion is the most-mentioned animal in the Bible; true or false?

ANSWERS: PAGE 348

Food & Drink
Kedgeree is made with rice and which other main ingredient?

Natural World
The dappled-sky appearance of alto-cumulus clouds is often likened to which fish?

History
Where are the Tamil Tigers a militant separatist group?

Culture & Belief
What is the name of the recess in a mosque wall indicating the direction of Mecca?

Stage & Screen
How much did it cost to see a nickelodeon film?

Written Word
What bespectacled boy-wizard is a pupil at Hogwarts School of Witchcraft and Wizardry?

Music
Which former *Eastenders* actor reached the top 10 in 1975 with *The Ugly Duckling*?

Famous People
What famous Danish storyteller wrote *The Ugly Duckling*?

Sport & Leisure
Whose ears did Mike Tyson bite during a fight?

Science & Tech
Which number appears on the top right of a push button phone?

True or False?
Images of St Peter normally depict the saint holding a fishing net; true or false?

ANSWERS: PAGE 349

Food & Drink
What colour is saffron?

 Natural World
What colour is malachite?

 History
Which two airlines merged to become British Airways?

 Culture & Belief
How would a newly-minted 2p coin differ from the original 2p coins?

 Stage & Screen
What palace did the BBC originally broadcast its TV programmes from?

 Written Word
In Scrabble, which letters are worth 8 points?

 Music
Which is the deepest-toned bass instrument?

 Famous People
How did Blondin cross Niagara Falls?

 Sport & Leisure
Which sportswear company is the brand with the three stripes?

 Science & Tech
What type of bridge is the Forth Road Bridge?

True or False?
In Venezuela, pink envelopes are charged half the usual postage; true or false?

ANSWERS: PAGE 349

Food & Drink Can you name one of the South American countries where potatoes were first cultivated?

 Natural World Which two countries border on Uruguay?

 History What Latin-American state was ruled by the Somoza dictatorship?

 Culture & Belief What is the church festival celebrated on 6 January, Twelfth Day?

 Stage & Screen Where in a theatre would you find barn doors?

 Written Word Flaubert said 'You can calculate the worth of a man by the number of his ...' what?

 Music Which well-known jazz musician presents the Radio 4 show *I'm Sorry, I Haven't a Clue*?

 Famous People Which performer's real name was Ehrich Weiss?

 Sport & Leisure Who won the rugby union World Cup in 1987?

 Science & Tech Chester Carbon devised the first of which now common office machine?

 True or False? An ostrich's eye is bigger than its brain; true or false?

ANSWERS: PAGE 350

Food & Drink
What kind of nuts are also known as filberts?

 Natural World
What river is the Isis better known as?

 History
Juan and Eva Peron ruled which country in 1946?

 Culture & Belief
What year in the Gregorian calendar is equal to 5760 in the Jewish calendar?

 Stage & Screen
What motel was the setting for a long-running TV soap in the 1960s?

 Written Word
Who is the private detective hero of books by Raymond Chandler?

 Music
Harry Chapin sang about a DJ on what radio station?

 Famous People
Who was the tallest president of the USA?

 Sport & Leisure
Where is the German motor racing Grand Prix held?

 Science & Tech
What is the SI unit of electric resistance?

True or False?
Jerome K. Jerome's middle initial was short for Kevin; true or false?

ANSWERS: PAGE 350

Food & Drink
In an average serving, which commonly eaten food has the highest iron content?

Natural World
Which city is also known informally as 'The Rock'?

History
Who was the Argentinian military leader at the time of the Falklands War?

Culture & Belief
Which architect said 'A house is a machine for living in'?

Stage & Screen
What street do TV's *Neighbours* live on?

Written Word
What American author was acquitted after he shot dead his wife in a William Tell-style stunt?

Music
What soul pairing duetted on *Endless Love* in 1981?

Famous People
How is architect and designer Charles Edward Jeanneret better known?

Sport & Leisure
What sport would you see at Hickstead?

Science & Tech
In the imperial system, how many gallons were in a peck?

True or False?
Peking was the first city to have a population of a million; true or false?

ANSWERS: PAGE 351

Food & Drink

What is the chemical name for vinegar?

Natural World

Which is the largest lake in the USA?

History

In 1984, who was assassinated by her Sikh bodyguards?

Culture & Belief

If the most able rule in a meritocracy, who rule in a gynocracy?

Stage & Screen

Where was Rick's Café?

Written Word

Babycakes was the fourth book in what televised series by Armistead Maupin?

Music

How many ways did Paul Simon sing of leaving your lover?

Famous People

Which Greek philosopher argued that since movement exists, there must be a god causing movement?

Sport & Leisure

Which golf major did Arnold Palmer fail to win?

Science & Tech

How many sheets of A4 paper could be cut from one sheet of A0?

True or False?

Cows have two stomachs; true or false?

ANSWERS: PAGE 351

Food & Drink
What is muscovado?

Natural World
How are the Sandwich Islands now known?

History
How was Indira Gandhi related to Mahatma Gandhi?

Culture & Belief
What pet name for a dog is Latin for 'I trust'?

Stage & Screen
What cities did Morse, Taggart and Van der Valk police?

Written Word
Who wrote the lines 'Don't follow leaders, watch parkin' meters'?

Music
What country was the birthplace of Chopin?

Famous People
How did Boadicea die?

Sport & Leisure
When Boris Becker was the first unseeded player to win Wimbledon, who did he beat in the final?

Science & Tech
What method of transport did Christopher Cockerell invent?

True or False?
A rhino's horn is actually made of compacted hair; true or false?

ANSWERS: PAGE 352

Food & Drink
Which pudding comes from the root of the cassava plant?

 Natural World
What constellation are the stars Castor and Pollux in?

 History
How long did the first circumnavigation of the earth via the two poles take?

 Culture & Belief
What do Americans call an apartment with two floors?

 Stage & Screen
What cities are home to the Abbey, Citizens and Crucible theatres?

 Written Word
What historic event took place at midnight in the book *Midnight's Children*?

 Music
Which number was Schubert's Unfinished Symphony?

 Famous People
What did Howard Carter and the Earl of Carnarvon find in 1922?

 Sport & Leisure
What adjective is used to describe Goodwood Racecourse?

 Science & Tech
In 1962, which train made its centenary journey?

True or False?
The first powered flight by the Wright brothers lasted for 62 seconds; true or false?

ANSWERS: PAGE 352

Food & Drink
Sailors combated which disease with limes for vitamin C?

 Natural World
The mistral winds blow from which mountains?

 History
In 1971 east Pakistan became which independent nation?

 Culture & Belief
Where about your person might you find a hologram of William Shakespeare?

 Stage & Screen
Liberty Bell was the signature tune for what completely different comedy show in the 1960s?

 Written Word
Which Scottish loch is the setting for Sir Walter Scott's *The Lady of the Lake*?

 Music
Which singer had the most hits without ever reaching number 1?

 Famous People
Who was the American rock star injured in Eddie Cochrane's fatal 1960 car crash?

 Sport & Leisure
What is the perfect score in ten-pin bowling?

 Science & Tech
How would you describe an iron bucket coated in zinc?

 True or False?
The actor Nicholas Cage is the nephew of director Francis Ford Coppola; true or false?

ANSWERS: PAGE 353

Food & Drink
What is cous-cous made from?

 Natural World
In what general direction do trade winds blow?

 History
Who was India's first prime minister?

 Culture & Belief
Which weekday did the Romans call 'dies jouis' or Jupiter's day?

 Stage & Screen
Who is Betty Perske better known as?

 Written Word
Which comedian said 'Gee, dat day Ah read a book – some day Ah'm gonna do it again'?

 Music
Which song kept Engelbert Humperdinck in the charts for over a year?

 Famous People
Lady Emma Hamilton had a daughter, Horatia. Who was the father?

 Sport & Leisure
Who was the first British golfer to win the US Masters at Augusta?

 Science & Tech
What does an orrery illustrate in model form?

True or False?
One of Germany's brewing laws regulates the diameter of bubbles in lager; true or false?

ANSWERS: PAGE 353

Food & Drink What type of cheese is traditionally associated with Greek salad?

 Natural World Which is furthest north between Alicante, Majorca and Ibiza?

 History Whose affair with Katharine O'Shea led to the end of his political career?

 Culture & Belief How many pounds does the slang term 'a monkey' mean?

 Stage & Screen Which is the odd one out: Snowy, Roobarb and Felix?

 Written Word What TV host said of his *Unreliable Memoirs* 'nothing is factual except the bits that sound like fiction'?

 Music What word described Lips Inc's town, the Goodies' gibbon and Jasper Carrot's moped?

 Famous People Who was the first Tudor king of England?

 Sport & Leisure Bishen Bedi was a spin bowler, taking 266 test wickets for which country?

 Science & Tech What would astonomers measure in parsecs?

 True or False? Edinburgh has the oldest university in Scotland; true or false?

ANSWERS: PAGE 354

Food & Drink
What shape of pasta would you expect if you asked for conchiglie?

Natural World
In which hemisphere is the Amundsen Sea?

History
What are the Netherlands East Indies now known as?

Culture & Belief
Which island parliament is composed of the Upper House and the House of Keys?

Stage & Screen
What 1960s kids' TV show, set on an African nature reserve, featured a cross-eyed lion called Clarence?

Written Word
'Publish and be sued' was the motto of what magazine's former editor?

Music
Which two types of instrument are played in Japanese *noh* drama?

Famous People
Which planet did Sir William Herschel discover in 1781?

Sport & Leisure
What is umpire Dickie Bird's real name?

Science & Tech
Where were the Royal Botanic Gardens founded in 1759?

True or False?
Lenin was the first president of the USSR; true or false?

ANSWERS: PAGE 354

Food & Drink How long does it take for one unit of alcohol to leave the body?

Natural World How many stars appear on the state flag of Texas?

History Who was elected Richard Nixon's vice-president?

Culture & Belief What country features the chrysanthemum on its imperial crest?

Stage & Screen What were the wars being fought in *The Green Berets*, *The Blue Max* and *Cross Of Iron*?

Written Word Whose poems of obituary in *Private Eye* invariably begin: 'So, farewell then…'?

Music Between July 1964 and August 1966, how many consecutive number 1s did the Beatles have?

Famous People Who painted *The Monarch of the Glen* and designed the lions in Trafalgar Square?

Sport & Leisure The bodyline method of bowling was introduced to combat which Australian?

Science & Tech Which Scottish railway station was named after a now-closed sewing machine factory?

True or False? Stirling Moss never won the world motor racing championship; true or false?

ANSWERS: PAGE 355

Food & Drink
Which county is Eccles, home of the cakes, in?

Natural World
What is the first animal mentioned in English dictionaries?

History
What was Gorbachev's policy of internal openness called?

Culture & Belief
Who were the opposing sides in the Battle of Naseby in 1645?

Stage & Screen
Who played the part of the Sorcerer's Apprentice in Disney's *Fantasia*?

Written Word
Whose travel book *Notes from a Small Island* was a runaway success in the UK?

Music
How many years apart were David Bowie's two chart entries with *Space Oddity*?

Famous People
Which Italian city is the home of Leonardo da Vinci's *Last Supper*?

Sport & Leisure
Who, in 1978, was the first player to score a century and take eight wickets in a test?

Science & Tech
Which cotton fabric was originally made at Calicut in India?

True or False?
Thomas Edison, pioneer of electricity, helped design the electric chair; true or false?

ANSWERS: PAGE 355

Food & Drink
On a bottle of HP sauce, what does HP stand for?

Natural World
What family of fish does the anchovy belong to?

History
When was the Berlin Wall built?

Culture & Belief
In heraldry, what word describes an animal with its front legs raised one above the other?

Stage & Screen
If Clint Eastwood was the Good and Lee van Cleef the Bad, who was the Ugly?

Written Word
What type of books did Winston Churchill think it good for an uneducated man to read?

Music
Who is the only artist to spend more than 1,000 weeks on the UK singles chart?

Famous People
Who was the Republican candidate beaten in the 1960 presidential election by John F. Kennedy?

Sport & Leisure
Which team holds the record for most consecutive wins of cricket's County Championship?

Science & Tech
The first zip fasteners were designed for doing up which items of clothing?

True or False?
Panama hats originated in Panama; true or false?

ANSWERS: PAGE 356

Food & Drink What would you put in Russian tea instead of milk?

 Natural World What season begins with the vernal equinox?

 History In what year did the Falklands War take place?

 Culture & Belief When did the union of Great Britain and Ireland come into force?

 Stage & Screen What was the relationship between Luke Skywalker and Princess Leia in *Star Wars*?

 Written Word Which character, when asked who made her, replied 'Nobody... I s'pect I just grow'd'?

 Music Who appears on the cover of Roxy Music's *Siren* album?

 Famous People Samuel Pepys' diaries recorded events in which decade?

 Sport & Leisure How does a test match cricketer qualify for the primary club?

 Science & Tech In 1947 an American pilot coined which phrase for unidentified flying objects?

 True or False? Raith Rovers Football Club's home town is Kirkcaldy; true or false?

ANSWERS: PAGE 356

Food & Drink How much milk does it take to make a pound of cheese?

 Natural World What are the two main metals combined to make bronze?

 History Where did the Americans' abortive invasion of Cuba take place?

 Culture & Belief Until 1836, there were only six universities in Britain: Oxford, Cambridge and which other four?

 Stage & Screen Who originally presented *Juke Box Jury*?

 Written Word Which Shakespeare character says 'But soft! What light through yonder window breaks'?

 Music Who composed the opera *Lakme* and the ballet *Coppelia*?

 Famous People Tony Blair became the fourth post-war Labour prime minister. Who were the other three?

 Sport & Leisure Which cricket side won the first ever County Championship and Sunday League double?

 Science & Tech Which peasant group destroyed machinery which they feared would destroy their livelihood?

 True or False? Ferdinand Magellan was Spanish; true or false?

ANSWERS: PAGE 357

Food & Drink
What type of flower is the source of vanilla?

 Natural World
What river are the Victoria Falls on?

 History
What three statesmen met at the peace conference at Yalta in 1945?

 Culture & Belief
The silver hallmark of a harp and crown belongs to which city?

 Stage & Screen
Which actor played James Bond for only one film?

 Written Word
'Reader, I married him.' Who was the 'I' in this marriage?

 Music
What instrument is associated with Pablo Cassals?

 Famous People
What did the 'D' stand for in Franklin D. Roosevelt's name?

 Sport & Leisure
What was Sir Len Hutton's two-innings total on his test debut?

 Science & Tech
Chirognomy attempts to read the character from which physical feature?

True or False?
Eboracum was the name the Romans give Lincoln; true or false?

ANSWERS: PAGE 357

Food & Drink
What rays are used in the irradiation of food to preserve it?

Natural World
So-called 'mermaids' purses' found on beaches are in fact the egg cases of which fish?

History
What three statesmen met in peace conference at Potsdam in 1945?

Culture & Belief
If a person dies intestate, what have they not done?

Stage & Screen
What city's film festival awards the Golden Bear?

Written Word
What is the better known nickname of Jame Gatz?

Music
What was jazz musician John Birks Gillespie's nickname?

Famous People
Between Gilbert and Sullivan, who wrote the music?

Sport & Leisure
Where is the Gadaffi stadium cricket ground?

Science & Tech
What measure of liquid equals 10lbs weight of distilled water?

True or False?
The source of the River Rhine is in Austria; true or false?

ANSWERS: PAGE 358

Food & Drink
Which spreadable foodstuff was invented during the Franco-Prussian War?

Natural World
On average, how much urine does an adult pass in 24 hours, to the nearest 100ml?

History
Who coined the phrase 'the iron curtain' to describe the division between east and west Europe?

Culture & Belief
Which country is represented in international vehicle registrations by the letter E?

Stage & Screen
What was Lovejoy's profession?

Written Word
What was Miss Marple's first name?

Music
The Stranglers had 96, but the Goombay Dance Band only had 7; of what?

Famous People
Leo Tolstoy, author of *War and Peace*, fought in what 19th-century war?

Sport & Leisure
How many balls start a game of snooker?

Science & Tech
If someone has the initials BDS after their name, what is their profession?

True or False?
Females have two X chromosomes; true or false?

ANSWERS: PAGE 358

Which animal's milk is used to make roquefort cheese?

 In which year did Hillary and Tenzing climb Everest?

 What line of fortifications did France build to protect its eastern border?

 What is the modern Polish name for the city of Danzig?

 What style of film-making was pioneered by John Grierson?

 James Joyce's *Ulysses* describes a day in the life of what Dublin character?

 In *Three Steps to Heaven*, what is step one?

 Which famous tenor was born in Naples in 1873?

 Who were the first two men to win world professional titles at snooker and billiards?

 What does a red fire extinguisher contain?

 Ireland became a republic in 1922; true or false?

ANSWERS: PAGE 359

Food & Drink What type of soft cheese was traditionally made from buffaloes' milk?

 Natural World Who does fratricide involve killing?

 History What does the name 'Bolsheviks' mean?

 Culture & Belief If an MBE is a member of the order of the British Empire, what is an OBE?

 Stage & Screen Where was the first-ever film festival held?

 Written Word *The Two Towers* is the second book in which trilogy?

 Music What, according to Ian Dury, is Wee Willie Harris?

 Famous People Which Italian is celebrated by an American public holiday on 12 October?

 Sport & Leisure Which three modern-day players have each won the world professional snooker championship 6 times?

 Science & Tech The members of New York's Diners Club were the first to own what item?

True or False? Tony Blair was once the long-haired lead singer with a student rock band; true or false?

ANSWERS: PAGE 359

Food & Drink
Which Italian city does parmesan cheese come from?

Natural World
What are Biscay, Trafalgar, Fastnet and German Bight?

History
When did Russia withdraw from the First World War?

Culture & Belief
Which workers can join the ASLEF union?

Stage & Screen
What record-breaking film marked Clint Eastwood's directorial debut?

Written Word
What are Times, Courier and Garamond examples of?

Music
How many quavers make a crotchet?

Famous People
Who is missing from this sequence: Fisher, Ramsay, Coggan, ..., Carey?

Sport & Leisure
What does Len Ganley referee?

Science & Tech
What does SCUBA stand for?

True or False?
Postboxes in Spain are yellow; true or false?

ANSWERS: PAGE 360

Food & Drink
Which crop is threatened by the Colorado beetle?

Natural World
What river does the Hoover Dam stand on?

History
What did Captain Robert Jenkins display in London in 1738, leading to a war with Spain?

Culture & Belief
On the Queen's coat of arms, which country is represented by the unicorn?

Stage & Screen
Who was Isabella Rossellini's famous mother?

Written Word
In which three successive years in the 1950s was *Lord of the Rings* published in three parts?

Music
What is a violinist's bow string made of?

Famous People
Which wit declared that 'Nothing succeeds like excess'?

Sport & Leisure
Who, in 1970, was the first Briton for 50 years to win the US Golf Open?

Science & Tech
How would the police catch a criminal using dactylography?

True or False?
Sir Walter Raleigh was responsible for introducing the potato to Britain; true or false?

ANSWERS: PAGE 360

Food & Drink
What are Kerr's Pinks and Maris Pipers?

Natural World
If hens sit on their eggs for three weeks, how long do swans sit on theirs?

History
When were British women given equal voting rights to men?

Culture & Belief
Which 13th-century saint's followers were known as the Grey Friars?

Stage & Screen
Which famous dancer directed the film *Hello Dolly*?

Written Word
Which American author has written extensively about everyday life in Lake Wobegon?

Music
What colour is common to hits by Fleetwood Mac, The Lemon Pipers and Shakin' Stevens?

Famous People
Which star of the Kirov ballet defected in 1979?

Sport & Leisure
What sport would you play with a mashie?

Science & Tech
Chuck Yeager was the first pilot to break what?

True or False?
All horses have the same official birthday; true or false?

ANSWERS: PAGE 361

Food & Drink
What vegetable is vodka sometimes made from?

Natural World
Grilse are young of which fish?

History
The colony at Botany Bay led to the establishment of which city?

Culture & Belief
What is the ancient language used in Buddhist ceremonies?

Stage & Screen
What acting first was bestowed on Henry Irving in 1895?

Written Word
William Donaldson wrote spoof letters to celebrities using what pseudonym?

Music
What was the avaricious-sounding subtitle of the Pet Shop Boys' hit *Opportunities*?

Famous People
What did William Wilberforce fight in Parliament to abolish?

Sport & Leisure
Who played golf on the moon?

Science & Tech
What fastening was inspired by observations of burdock seeds clinging to clothes?

True or False?
Sex was the 'original sin' that had Adam and Eve expelled from the Garden of Eden; true or false?

ANSWERS: PAGE 361

Food & Drink
What useful digestive function do the leaves and pods of the senna plant perform?

Natural World
Which northern Scottish island gave its name to a style of pullover?

History
What were the three estates traditionally seen as making up the medieval kingdom?

Culture & Belief
The Royal Company of Archers serve as the Queen's bodyguard in which country?

Stage & Screen
Which actor appeared as Ivanhoe, The Saint and James Bond?

Written Word
After Bonkers the dog bit Garp's ear, how did Garp get his own back?

Music
Deacon Blue took their name from a track by which band?

Famous People
Derek Hatton was a councillor in which English city?

Sport & Leisure
Royal Blackheath is the oldest what in England?

Science & Tech
Which two architectural orders are combined in the composite order?

True or False?
The term 'Art Deco' came into use in the mid 1920s; true or false?

ANSWERS: PAGE 362

Food & Drink — What is sodium chloride more commonly known as?

Natural World — What small aquatic creature has the Latin name *hippocampus*?

History — The name of an art movement, what does the word 'dada' mean?

Culture & Belief — Helvetia is the Latin name for what country?

Stage & Screen — Where did the first cinema in the UK open?

Written Word — What Greek letter has come to mean a very small amount?

Music — Which musical impresario had hits as Bubblerock, Sakkarin, Shag and 100 Ton and a Feather?

Famous People — Who was the last English monarch to remain unmarried throughout their reign?

Sport & Leisure — Who played in the longest ever Wimbledon match?

Science & Tech — Where in a classroom might you see Mercator's Projection?

True or False? — The zodiac sign of Aquarius has the amethyst as its birth stone; true or false?

ANSWERS: PAGE 362

Food & Drink
What is the difference between oil and fat?

 Natural World
What river flows into the sea at New York?

 History
Who wrote the imperialist poem *The White Man's Burden* in 1899?

 Culture & Belief
Which Irish town gives its name to a five-line poem?

 Stage & Screen
In what year did the number of colour films released in Britain first exceed the black and white ones?

 Written Word
The film *Schindler's List* was based on which book by Thomas Keneally?

 Music
What 1970s band included guitarists Overend Watts and Ariel Bender?

 Famous People
In what year did Louis Bleriot become the first person to fly across the English Channel?

 Sport & Leisure
In what sport would you perform a christie?

 Science & Tech
Which company sold the first instant coffee?

 True or False?
The maximum number of times a piece of paper can be folded in half is seven; true or false?

ANSWERS: PAGE 363

Food & Drink
What type of tree is the source of sago?

 Natural World
Peruvian guano was first used as a fertilizer in the 1840s. What is guano?

 History
What century saw the end of the Chinese Ming dynasty?

 Culture & Belief
In Scandinavian mythology whose souls went to Valhalla?

 Stage & Screen
What film did Charlie Chaplin first speak in?

 Written Word
What is the subject of Horace McCoy's *They Shoot Horses, Don't They*?

 Music
Who was the bald-headed singer in Classix Nouveau?

 Famous People
Alfred the Great founded which one of the three modern-day armed services?

 Sport & Leisure
Which sport is played for the Davis Cup?

 Science & Tech
What was made by the Manhattan Project?

True or False?
A dowry was originally brought to a marriage by the male partner; true or false?

ANSWERS: PAGE 363

Food & Drink
Which bottled water used the advertising slogan 'L'eau and behold'?

 Natural World
What Scottish region is Gretna Green in?

 History
Which sultanate and empire was known in the 19th and early 20th centuries as the 'sick man of Europe'?

 Culture & Belief
Terence Rattigan dedicated *The Winslow Boy* to which boy who later became one of Mrs Thatcher's cabinet?

 Stage & Screen
When did Superman first appear on TV (to within two years)?

 Written Word
In which year was Orwell's *1984* published?

 Music
Hamlet Cigars' adverts have become identified with which piece of music by J. S. Bach?

 Famous People
Name the city where David Dinkins was the first black mayor.

 Sport & Leisure
Which English football team dropped Woolwich from its name?

 Science & Tech
The first paper hankies, Celluwipes, were given which new name by manufacturers Kimberley-Clark?

 True or False?
Shredded Wheat was the first commercially produced breakfast cereal; true or false?

ANSWERS: PAGE 364

Food & Drink
Which drinks company sponsors the comedy award at the Edinburgh Festival Fringe?

Natural World
Of stalactites and stalagmites, which grow upwards?

History
What term was given to the ritual of prostrating oneself before the Chinese emperor?

Culture & Belief
Which low, stuffed seat with no back is named after the Turkish empire?

Stage & Screen
Which Hollywood superstar established the Sundance Institute to promote independent movie-making?

Written Word
Who wrote *Jaws*?

Music
Who was the long-tongued star of Bad Manners?

Famous People
Golfer Vijay Singh is a native of which country?

Sport & Leisure
Who was the last amateur to win the Open golf championship?

Science & Tech
From which phrase was the word 'radar' extracted?

True or False?
A Batmitzvah is the female equivalent of a Barmitzvah; true or false?

ANSWERS: PAGE 364

Food & Drink

Rickets is caused by a deficiency of which vitamin?

 Natural World

Phobos and Deimos are moons of which planet?

 History

George Bernard Shaw and H. G. Wells were members of which socialist group?

 Culture & Belief

Which country was Mikhail Baryshnikov in when he defected to the west?

 Stage & Screen

Jack Lemmon was one half of *The Odd Couple*; who was the other half?

 Written Word

How many husbands had Scarlett O'Hara before Rhett Butler?

 Music

Which 1980s band took their name from a tin of paint?

 Famous People

What was Oscar Wilde's second given name?

 Sport & Leisure

How many times did Sir Gordon Richards win the Derby?

 Science & Tech

What type of wind is represented by 12 on the Beaufort scale?

 True or False?

Boxer Joe Frazier was known as 'the Brown Bomber'; true or false?

ANSWERS: PAGE 365

Food & Drink
How do green vegetables differ from root vegetables?

Natural World
Which animal is a cross between a male ass and a female horse?

History
Who was the 'Sea-Green Incorruptible' who led the reign of terror in revolutionary France?

Culture & Belief
What was the difference between a highwayman and a footpad?

Stage & Screen
Which canine star left her prints on the cement outside Mann's Chinese Theater?

Written Word
Who is the Edinburgh detective created by author Ian Rankin?

Music
Who played Che Guevara in the original London cast of *Evita*?

Famous People
Whose gang were the perpetrators of the St Valentine's Day Massacre?

Sport & Leisure
In the 1970s, which horse racing trophy did Sagaro win three times?

Science & Tech
Which institutions benefit from using the Dewey decimal system?

True or False?
The original Greek Olympic Games took place every 10 years; true or false?

ANSWERS: PAGE 365

Food & Drink Who were known as TV's *Two Fat Ladies*?

 Natural World What is the main town of Jersey?

 History The Chrysler Airflow was a commercially unsuccessful but very influential design of what?

 Culture & Belief Ravi Shankar was an exponent of which musical instrument?

 Stage & Screen Who was the longest-serving Dr Who?

 Written Word What was W. Somerset Maugham's first name?

 Music What number overture was ELO's first hit?

 Famous People Which famous widow did Aristotle Onassis marry in 1968?

 Sport & Leisure Who, in 1977, was the first snooker player to win the World Championship with a two-piece cue?

 Science & Tech Which professional people might be fellows of the RIBA?

 True or False? A baby whale is called a foal; true or false?

ANSWERS: PAGE 366

Food & Drink Which has more calories, a pint of lager, a pint of cider or a can of coke?

 Natural World How would a python kill its prey?

 History In an essay in 1734, what did Alexander Pope say is the proper study of mankind?

 Culture & Belief Waitangi Day is a national holiday in which country?

 Stage & Screen What 1942 classic is the most frequently shown film on US TV?

 Written Word Who is the professor who narrates Nabokov's *Lolita*?

 Music Which singer/songwriter sang 'I'll have to say I love you in a song'?

 Famous People Who began in *The Sweeney* before graduating to Oxford as *Inspector Morse*?

 Sport & Leisure What was Ray Reardon's occupation before he became a snooker professional?

 Science & Tech What was the trademark name for the plastic resin developed by Leo Baekeland?

 True or False? A 50p piece has seven edges; true or false?

ANSWERS: PAGE 366

Food & Drink Which cooking ingredient was developed from the Paisley textile trade?

Natural World At what age do human males reach half their adult height?

History Which car manufacturer made the Anglia?

Culture & Belief How were the great plagues of the Middle Ages transmitted?

Stage & Screen Who or what was 'Alex' in the title of the film, *Ice Cold In Alex*?

Written Word Who wrote *Cat on a Hot Tin Roof*?

Music What was the Troggs' only number 1?

Famous People What title was held by Irish soldier and statesman Arthur Wellesley?

Sport & Leisure Which racecourse hosts the Scottish Grand National?

Science & Tech The first example of what device was fitted by Blaupunkt into a Studebaker?

True or False? The first car speedometers only went up to 35 mph; true or false?

ANSWERS: PAGE 367

Food & Drink

What would you buy from a bodega?

Natural World

What kind of creature is a flying fox?

History

What was the first successful English colony, commemorating Elizabeth I in its name?

Culture & Belief

What do we call the day before All Saints' Day?

Stage & Screen

Which actor, famous for playing Dracula, was born in Transylvania?

Written Word

Who wrote short stories called *A Perfect Day for Bananafish* and *For Esme, With Love and Squalor*?

Music

Who released a single in the shape of the African continent?

Famous People

How is Karol Wojtyla better known?

Sport & Leisure

Which racecourse is the home of the Kentucky Derby?

Science & Tech

What was a Stutz Bearcat?

True or False?

Model-T Fords were always black; true or false?

ANSWERS: PAGE 367

Food & Drink — What nut gives flavour to ratafia?

 Natural World — What is a young hare called?

 History — When was the Berlin Wall pulled down?

 Culture & Belief — Which symbol united the followers of York and Lancaster?

 Stage & Screen — Who was Emma Peel's replacement in the original *Avengers* TV series?

 Written Word — What does Holden Caulfield say he will be, in the title of a book by J. D. Salinger?

 Music — What, ironically, was the Rolling Stones' first number 1 hit?

 Famous People — Who was the second man to walk on the moon?

 Sport & Leisure — What major race is run at Longchamp?

 Science & Tech — Which speech from Shakespeare was recited on the first public demonstration of the telephone?

True or False? — There are 13 red and white stripes on the American flag; true or false?

ANSWERS: PAGE 368

Food & Drink — Which name, from an Italian city, is given to a two- or three-flavoured ice cream?

Natural World — Which island group includes Mallorca, Menorca and Ibiza?

History — Early digital watches featured LED displays. What does LED stand for?

Culture & Belief — Which Greek philosopher was taught by Socrates, and in turn taught Aristotle?

Stage & Screen — What cinematic award was originally nicknamed a Stella?

Written Word — How many lines are in a sonnet?

Music — Which opera features the *Toreador's Song*?

Famous People — Which entertainer insured his distinctive front teeth for £4million?

Sport & Leisure — At what distance was Roger Black British number one?

Science & Tech — Bell made the first long-distance telephone call in 1892 between which two American cities?

True or False? — Jim Clark was the first to win the world motor racing driver's championship posthumously; true or false?

ANSWERS: PAGE 368

Food & Drink — Which food manufacturer sponsors Norwich City FC?

 Natural World — Which stretch of water separates the Isle of Wight from the mainland?

 History — How far, to the nearest 10 metres, could a skilled medieval longbowman fire a deadly arrow?

 Culture & Belief — Who brought news to illiterate townspeople in past centuries?

 Stage & Screen — What does BAFTA stand for?

 Written Word — Which writer's first names are John Ronald Reuel?

 Music — What instruction was the title of Cliff Richard's first hit?

 Famous People — Where is Karl Marx buried?

 Sport & Leisure — Hakkinen and Coulthard drove for which Formula 1 team in 1998?

 Science & Tech — If contours connect points of equal height on a map, what do isobaths connect?

 True or False? — The French spirit Calvados is made from fermented apples; true or false?

ANSWERS: PAGE 369

Food & Drink
Fray Bentos is a port in which country?

Natural World
Niagara Falls is between which two Great Lakes?

History
How many pennies were in an old style British pound?

Culture & Belief
On a map of the London Underground, which line is coloured grey?

Stage & Screen
What now regular event took place at Hollywood's Roosevelt Hotel on 16 May 1929?

Written Word
According to Jeanette Winterson, what are oranges not?

Music
Johnny Wakelin had two hits with songs about which sportsman?

Famous People
What was army chaplain Geoffrey Anketell Studdert-Kennedy nicknamed for giving soldiers cigarettes?

Sport & Leisure
Which British sporting venue includes the Paddock Hill grandstand?

Science & Tech
What was the innovative feature of the Rolex 'Oyster' watch?

True or False?
By law, Scotch whisky must be left for five years after distilling before it can be sold; true or false?

ANSWERS: PAGE 369

Food & Drink
TVP is made from soya, but what does TVP stand for?

Natural World
What are the names of the two falls that make up Niagara?

History
Which company did a yellow bird called Busby advertise?

Culture & Belief
Which coin bears the phrase 'Standing on the shoulders of giants'?

Stage & Screen
How many members does the Academy of Motion Picture Arts and Sciences have (to the nearest 100)?

Written Word
In the books by P. G. Wodehouse, whose manservant is Jeeves?

Music
In the Elvis song, what was the name of his latest flame?

Famous People
What famous hotel is named after the founder of Singapore?

Sport & Leisure
Which card game features his heels and his nobs?

Science & Tech
What term was coined in 1937 to describe a stock of human blood for transfusions?

True or False?
Rembrandt painted *The Laughing Cavalier*; true or false?

ANSWERS: PAGE 370

Food & Drink

What ingredient forms the topping on crème brûlée?

Natural World

Which Scottish island group features Skara Brae, Scapa Flow and the Old Man of Hoy?

History

Whose first volume of war memoirs was called *Adolf Hitler: My Part in his Downfall?*

Culture & Belief

In pantomime, whose sweetheart was Columbine?

Stage & Screen

How tall, to the nearest inch, is an Oscar statuette?

Written Word

Who is the salesman in Arthur Miller's *Death of a Salesman*?

Music

Who wrote the Monkees' hit *I'm a Believer*?

Famous People

After the Vietnam war, what was the new name for Saigon?

Sport & Leisure

Donald and Malcolm Campbell both drove vehicles with which name?

Science & Tech

Which item of office stationery do the French call 'trombones'?

True or False?

The Smurfs were originally known as Les Schtroumpfs; true or false?

ANSWERS: PAGE 370

SECTION TWO

THE QUIZ BOOK ANSWERS

SETS 1 – 240

SET 1

Food & Drink	A poisoned apple
Natural World	Mad Cow Disease
History	Two
Culture & Belief	Eros
Stage & Screen	Four
Written Word	Melchester
Music	The road to Mandalay
Famous People	Arthur Miller and Marilyn Monroe
Sport & Leisure	For winning the US Masters and leading the Tour de France
Science & Tech	Stephen Hawking
True or False?	True

SET 2

Food & Drink	Manna
Natural World	Four inches
History	Caligula
Culture & Belief	Christian Dior
Stage & Screen	Z Cars
Written Word	The Canterbury Tales
Music	Beethoven
Famous People	Allan Pinkerton
Sport & Leisure	Kirkcaldy
Science & Tech	Karl Benz
True or False?	True

SET 3

Food & Drink	Juniper
Natural World	Chicago
History	To sound less German in WWI (it was a name-change)
Culture & Belief	Ecuador (they were shipped from Panama)
Stage & Screen	*North By Northwest*
Written Word	John Osborne
Music	Noel Gallagher
Famous People	Charles Darwin
Sport & Leisure	*Pot Black*
Science & Tech	On the side of a ship
True or False?	True

SET 4

Food & Drink	Fat
Natural World	The Negev
History	Almost 29 years (1961-89)
Culture & Belief	Quakers
Stage & Screen	*Snow White And The Seven Dwarfs*
Written Word	The four archangels
Music	Leon Trotsky
Famous People	Paul Keating
Sport & Leisure	New Zealand
Science & Tech	Albert Einstein
True or False?	False (it did in 1877)

SET 5

Food & Drink	A cheese	Written Word	Erskine Childers
Natural World	The Northern Lights	Music	*Reasons To Be Cheerful, Part 3*
History	None	Famous People	Aviation
Culture & Belief	The Ten Commandments	Sport & Leisure	The Jules Rimet Trophy
Stage & Screen	Charlton Heston	Science & Tech	The de Haviland Comet
		True or False?	True (in 1892)

SET 6

Food & Drink	Smash Instant Mashed Potato	Written Word	Silas Marner
Natural World	Aurora australis	Music	A miner 49-er
History	26	Famous People	Work
Culture & Belief	Drink from it	Sport & Leisure	1972
Stage & Screen	The nickname of India's film industry	Science & Tech	Dynamite
		True or False?	False (the Queen has no passport)

SET 7

Food & Drink	Turmeric
Natural World	The River Nile
History	Julius Caesar
Culture & Belief	15th March
Stage & Screen	Jacques Cousteau's

Written Word	Ophelia
Music	Richie Valens and The Big Bopper
Famous People	Wallis Simpson
Sport & Leisure	100 m, 200 m, 4 x 100 m relay, Long Jump
Science & Tech	Jacques Cousteau
True or False?	False

SET 8

Food & Drink	Herring
Natural World	Pennsylvania
History	Sarajevo
Culture & Belief	Capricorn
Stage & Screen	*Pinky And Perky*

Written Word	Ebenezer Scrooge
Music	Pete Best
Famous People	Walt Disney
Sport & Leisure	Thomas Lord (its developer)
Science & Tech	All known chemical elements
True or False?	True

SET 9

Food & Drink	Bitter

Natural World	The intestines of sheep

History	Abraham Lincoln

Culture & Belief	Demons and goblins

Stage & Screen	Scott, Virgil, Alan, Gordon, John

Written Word	Mycroft

Music	*Flowers In The Rain* (by The Move)

Famous People	All were assassinated

Sport & Leisure	India

Science & Tech	The Morris Mini

True or False?	False (all are types of knot)

SET 10

Food & Drink	Haggis

Natural World	A reindeer

History	1863

Culture & Belief	The pope

Stage & Screen	Fred Astaire and Ginger Rogers

Written Word	Salome

Music	Tennessee

Famous People	All were left handed

Sport & Leisure	35-1

Science & Tech	Uranus

True or False?	False (there are 9)

SET 11

Food & Drink	Ham and cheese
Natural World	A meteor
History	The Library of Alexandria
Culture & Belief	£50
Stage & Screen	Toto
Written Word	Manchester
Music	Louis Armstrong
Famous People	Satchel-mouth
Sport & Leisure	Kenneth Wolstenholme (at the World Cup Final)
Science & Tech	By being the first woman in space
True or False?	True

SET 12

Food & Drink	Beans Means Heinz
Natural World	The River Nile
History	Countess Constance Markievicz (in 1918)
Culture & Belief	St Valentine
Stage & Screen	George C. Scott and Marlon Brando
Written Word	Billy Bunter
Music	T'Pau
Famous People	Louis XIV (by 8 years)
Sport & Leisure	Dennis Taylor
Science & Tech	The Humber Bridge
True or False?	True

SET 13

| Food & Drink | Honey |

| Written Word | Harry Lime |

| Music | *Rockin' All Over The World* (by Status Quo) |

| Natural World | K2 |

| Famous People | Orson Welles' |

| History | The First World War ended |

| Sport & Leisure | Uruguay (in 1930) |

| Culture & Belief | Ten |

| Science & Tech | John Glenn |

| Stage & Screen | Fred Astaire |

| True or False? | True |

SET 14

| Food & Drink | Jerusalem artichokes |

| Written Word | Matt Groening |

| Music | The Chieftains |

| Natural World | Shipping areas |

| Famous People | Canterbury Cathedral |

| History | James VI of Scotland and I of England |

| Sport & Leisure | Scrabble |

| Culture & Belief | So be it |

| Science & Tech | Just over 8 minutes |

| Stage & Screen | Celia Johnson and Trevor Howard |

| True or False? | True |

SET 15

Food & Drink — In a hot dog roll

Natural World — Texas

History — Lady Jane Grey (queen for 10 days)

Culture & Belief — The Koran

Stage & Screen — The 4th of July

Written Word — Superman (by 11 months)

Music — The Jordanaires

Famous People — US President Theodore Roosevelt

Sport & Leisure — A pack of cards

Science & Tech — Your knee-cap

True or False? — False

SET 16

Food & Drink — Coca-Cola

Natural World — Canberra

History — The Confederacy

Culture & Belief — Hope

Stage & Screen — *St Elmo's Fire*

Written Word — Smallville

Music — Wagner

Famous People — Andrew Carnegie

Sport & Leisure — Weightlifting

Science & Tech — DNA

True or False? — False

SET 17

Food & Drink	A lemon
Natural World	Greenland
History	Seven
Culture & Belief	25th March, year 0
Stage & Screen	*The White Horses*
Written Word	George Orwell
Music	Both had hits with *Amazing Grace*
Famous People	Václav Havel
Sport & Leisure	Scotland and England
Science & Tech	The structure of DNA
True or False?	True

SET 18

Food & Drink	Marie Antoinette
Natural World	Vatican City
History	Hyde Park
Culture & Belief	Taoism
Stage & Screen	Mr Benn
Written Word	Lewis Carroll
Music	New York
Famous People	Andy Warhol
Sport & Leisure	Tourist Trophy
Science & Tech	Pasteurisation
True or False?	False

SET 19

Food & Drink
Whisky (meaning 'water of life')

Natural World
Poland

History
The Great Exhibition of 1851

Culture & Belief
The Mormon Church

Stage & Screen
Weatherfield

Written Word
George Bernard Shaw

Music
Harry Lauder

Famous People
Buzz Aldrin

Sport & Leisure
Trevor Francis

Science & Tech
Each was named after its inventor

True or False?
True

SET 20

Food & Drink
In meat pies (his neighbour was a baker)

Natural World
None (they are two names for the same animal)

History
Franklin D. Roosevelt

Culture & Belief
Haile Selassie

Stage & Screen
The Archers

Written Word
How To Win Friends & Influence People

Music
Sarah Brightman

Famous People
Florence Nightingale

Sport & Leisure
47 minutes

Science & Tech
1001

True or False?
False

SET 21

| Written Word | Ronald Reagan |

| Food & Drink | Aubergine |

| Music | Simon Rattle |

| Natural World | The fast speed of its beating wings |

| Famous People | Charles Stewart Parnell |

| History | Richard Cromwell |

| Sport & Leisure | 1984 (Los Angeles) |

| Culture & Belief | Hinduism |

| Science & Tech | Rust |

| Stage & Screen | The Archers |

| True or False? | False (it is Mandarin) |

SET 22

| Written Word | Bash Street |

| Food & Drink | Sherry |

| Music | *Galway Bay* |

| Natural World | 20,000 |

| Famous People | Roald Amundsen |

| History | The crown jewels |

| Sport & Leisure | Joe Di Maggio |

| Culture & Belief | The pyramids of Egypt |

| Science & Tech | 90 degrees |

| Stage & Screen | *Catweazle* |

| True or False? | False |

SET 23

| Written Word | The Barretts |

| Food & Drink | A folded-over pizza |

| Music | A septet |

| Natural World | Cape Town |

| Famous People | Uri Geller |

| History | His arm |

| Sport & Leisure | Boris Becker |

| Culture & Belief | Chinese culture |

| Science & Tech | 1919 |

| Stage & Screen | *Eldorado* |

| True or False? | True |

SET 24

| Written Word | C. S. Lewis |

| Food & Drink | Robert Louis Stevenson |

| Music | The Overlanders |

| Natural World | Feign death to fool your opponent |

| Famous People | Paul Revere |

| History | George VI |

| Sport & Leisure | Samuel Beckett |

| Culture & Belief | In the centre (it is where the congregation sits) |

| Science & Tech | Helium |

| Stage & Screen | *Camberwick Green* |

| True or False? | True |

SET 25

| Food & Drink | Potatoes |

| Natural World | A blue whale calf |

| History | 4 July 1976 |

| Culture & Belief | Abel |

| Stage & Screen | Eugene O'Neill |

| Written Word | Wilfred Owen |

| Music | Billy Ocean |

| Famous People | Madonna |

| Sport & Leisure | Jamaica |

| Science & Tech | The compact disc |

| True or False? | False (it blooms every 10-30 years) |

SET 26

| Food & Drink | Prawns |

| Natural World | Istanbul |

| History | US troops in Britain in WWII |

| Culture & Belief | David |

| Stage & Screen | Flipper and Skippy |

| Written Word | Gnasher |

| Music | Andy Stewart |

| Famous People | Oscar Wilde |

| Sport & Leisure | Athens (in 1896) |

| Science & Tech | Viruses |

| True or False? | True |

SET 27

Food & Drink	The Greek gods
Natural World	Nepal
History	Culloden
Culture & Belief	Coca-Cola's
Stage & Screen	Tennessee Williams
Written Word	*A La Recherche Du Temps Perdu* (by Marcel Proust)
Music	Blur
Famous People	Billy Graham
Sport & Leisure	22
Science & Tech	32
True or False?	False (it was curry)

SET 28

Food & Drink	A marinated herring
Natural World	The Great Wall of China
History	The IRA (after the Brighton bombing)
Culture & Belief	King Arthur
Stage & Screen	The Capulets
Written Word	King Arthur
Music	Eric Clapton
Famous People	Little
Sport & Leisure	The British Empire Games
Science & Tech	The gluteus maximus
True or False?	True

SET 29

Food & Drink	Lemon

Natural World	The USSR

History	The Order of the Garter

Culture & Belief	Buddha

Stage & Screen	*Breakfast At Tiffany's*

Written Word	Big Ears

Music	Eight maids a-milking

Famous People	Jean Harlow

Sport & Leisure	1968

Science & Tech	None (it is a bell)

True or False?	True

SET 30

Food & Drink	They are all champagne-bottle sizes

Natural World	Brambles

History	1968

Culture & Belief	Teacher

Stage & Screen	Cap. Jean-Luc Picard (in *Star Trek: The Next Generation*)

Written Word	12

Music	Luciano Pavarotti, José Carreras and Placido Domingo

Famous People	Marilyn Monroe

Sport & Leisure	Princess Anne

Science & Tech	Albert Einstein

True or False?	True

SET 31

Food & Drink	Garibaldi
Natural World	Everything
History	Alaska
Culture & Belief	One (French)
Stage & Screen	Father Ted

Written Word	Walter Scott
Music	*The Gambler*
Famous People	Fidel Castro
Sport & Leisure	Bjorn Borg
Science & Tech	$22/7$
True or False?	False (it was a chair-back cover)

SET 32

Food & Drink	Picnic baskets
Natural World	A depression or low
History	One
Culture & Belief	A US dollar bill
Stage & Screen	He is an android

Written Word	Flo
Music	Daniel Barenboim
Famous People	Mother Theresa of Calcutta
Sport & Leisure	The High Jump
Science & Tech	Robert Oppenheimer
True or False?	True

SET 33

Food & Drink	Beer
Natural World	Cirrus
History	Suffragettes
Culture & Belief	Esso's
Stage & Screen	*Cabaret*
Written Word	Yukio Mishima
Music	Pluck
Famous People	July
Sport & Leisure	The Harlem Globetrotters
Science & Tech	The elbow
True or False?	True

SET 34

Food & Drink	Anna Pavlova
Natural World	Approx. 3960 miles (6385 km)
History	The prime minister
Culture & Belief	Woodstock
Stage & Screen	Mulder and Scully
Written Word	*The Addams Family*
Music	Finger its holes to play notes
Famous People	Bonnie Prince Charlie
Sport & Leisure	The Triathlon
Science & Tech	Surgery
True or False?	False (it was 1914)

SET 35

Food & Drink	Locusts and wild honey	Written Word	Ursula Le Guin
Natural World	Fingerprints	Music	Babylon Zoo
History	Six	Famous People	William Randolph Hearst
Culture & Belief	St Augustine	Sport & Leisure	Yachting
Stage & Screen	Victor Meldrew	Science & Tech	212 degrees
		True or False?	True

SET 36

Food & Drink	Almond	Written Word	The Falklands War
Natural World	Lava is magma which comes onto the Earth's surface	Music	John Brown's
History	The Battle of Waterloo	Famous People	Ike Turner (she is Tina)
Culture & Belief	Christopher Wren	Sport & Leisure	Geoff Hurst
Stage & Screen	*Northern Exposure*	Science & Tech	Four
		True or False?	False (he only worked in South Africa)

SET 37

| Written Word | *Lord Of The Flies* |

| Food & Drink | Haggis |

| Music | The Kinks |

| Natural World | Four |

| Famous People | Che Guevara |

| History | Black and blue |

| Sport & Leisure | In the USA |

| Culture & Belief | Weatherman |

| Science & Tech | Too low |

| Stage & Screen | Emergency Room |

| True or False? | False (it is a region in Argentina) |

SET 38

| Written Word | In Xanadu |

| Food & Drink | Three years |

| Music | Giacomo Puccini |

| Natural World | Lakes |

| Famous People | Boadicea |

| History | William the Conqueror |

| Sport & Leisure | 2000 Guineas, Derby, St Leger |

| Culture & Belief | To show membership of a club |

| Science & Tech | The liver |

| Stage & Screen | Hopkirk was a ghost |

| True or False? | True |

SET 39

Food & Drink	Gelatine
Natural World	15 degrees
History	Albania
Culture & Belief	Scientology
Stage & Screen	*Cheers*

Written Word	Paris and London
Music	Garth Brooks
Famous People	Edward VII
Sport & Leisure	Featherweight
Science & Tech	Yeast
True or False?	True

SET 40

Food & Drink	Roast lamb
Natural World	ante meridiem and post meridiem
History	Damascus
Culture & Belief	Riverdance
Stage & Screen	*Friends*

Written Word	Oscar Wilde
Music	ABC
Famous People	Billy the Kid
Sport & Leisure	Bobby Jones
Science & Tech	Red
True or False?	False

SET 41

Food & Drink
Currency

Natural World
Australia and New Zealand

History
1984

Culture & Belief
The pope

Stage & Screen
Brideshead

Written Word
The Hitch-Hiker's Guide To The Galaxy

Music
Phil Lynott

Famous People
Pat Garrett

Sport & Leisure
All have hosted the Commonwealth Games

Science & Tech
Mercury

True or False?
False (the only one who did was Nixon)

SET 42

Food & Drink
Bread

Natural World
Aluminium

History
The *Titanic*

Culture & Belief
Martin Luther King

Stage & Screen
True Grit

Written Word
His pipe, bowl and fiddlers three

Music
Johnny Cash

Famous People
Andrew Carnegie

Sport & Leisure
London and Glasgow

Science & Tech
Two

True or False?
False

SET 43

Food & Drink	Months without an 'r' in them
Natural World	Chalk
History	1920s
Culture & Belief	240
Stage & Screen	*Dad's Army*

Written Word	He died
Music	*My Generation*
Famous People	David Lloyd George
Sport & Leisure	Basketball
Science & Tech	Atmosphere
True or False?	False

SET 44

Food & Drink	It is unleavened
Natural World	Winds
History	His right
Culture & Belief	Stephen
Stage & Screen	It was the first colour TV series

Written Word	A secret never to be told
Music	Culture Club
Famous People	F. W. Woolworth
Sport & Leisure	The F. A. Cup
Science & Tech	Twice the speed of sound
True or False?	False

SET 45

Food & Drink	Jonah
Natural World	Alaska
History	John F. Kennedy
Culture & Belief	Saatchi & Saatchi
Stage & Screen	Fay Wray
Written Word	It's the temperature books combust at
Music	Erasure
Famous People	Gerald Ford
Sport & Leisure	Pelota
Science & Tech	273.15
True or False?	True

SET 46

Food & Drink	It's raw
Natural World	The International Date Line
History	Tax evasion
Culture & Belief	Fair Isle knitwear
Stage & Screen	*Star Trek*
Written Word	Haggis
Music	Richie Valens, Los Lobos
Famous People	The Red Baron
Sport & Leisure	72
Science & Tech	Tin
True or False?	True

SET 47

Written Word	Three

| Food & Drink | Pea soup |

| Music | A cappella |

| Natural World | Fog |

| Famous People | Sleep (he suffered from insomnia) |

| History | Sitting Bull |

| Sport & Leisure | Polo |

| Culture & Belief | Quangos |

| Science & Tech | An imperial ton |

| Stage & Screen | Silver |

| True or False? | True |

SET 48

| Written Word | Arthur Miller |

| Food & Drink | Seaweed |

| Music | Elvis Presley (with 8 in 1957) |

| Natural World | 2062 |

| Famous People | George III |

| History | Britain (in the Boer War) |

| Sport & Leisure | Saïd Aouita |

| Culture & Belief | In the Old Testament |

| Science & Tech | An earthquake |

| Stage & Screen | *Steamboat Willie* |

| True or False? | True |

SET 49

Food & Drink	Texas
Natural World	The Navaho
History	A UFO
Culture & Belief	Baked earth
Stage & Screen	Corleone
Written Word	J. M. Synge
Music	*We Shall Overcome*
Famous People	Rasputin
Sport & Leisure	Lacrosse
Science & Tech	Upper arm bone and buttock muscle
True or False?	True

SET 50

Food & Drink	Oats
Natural World	The Angel Falls in Venezuela
History	Robert Peel
Culture & Belief	Paper money (it is a wallet)
Stage & Screen	They are uncle and nephew
Written Word	Mario Puzo
Music	*The Bells Of Hell*
Famous People	Lawrence of Arabia
Sport & Leisure	26 miles 385 yd
Science & Tech	60 degrees
True or False?	True

SET 51

Food & Drink	Cow pie
Natural World	The African elephant
History	Government Issue
Culture & Belief	St Swithin
Stage & Screen	*In Which We Serve*

Written Word	Brendan Behan
Music	A solo performance
Famous People	Vivienne Westwood
Sport & Leisure	A bamboo sword
Science & Tech	To prevent them freezing (it is anti-freeze)
True or False?	False (Scotch comes only from Scotland)

SET 52

Food & Drink	Sugar and spice and all things nice
Natural World	Thailand
History	China
Culture & Belief	A girl's coming of age
Stage & Screen	*Dr Zhivago*

Written Word	Robert Burns
Music	*Carmen*
Famous People	Henry Ford
Sport & Leisure	Ice
Science & Tech	A nautical mile
True or False?	False (it is a 12-sided regular polygon)

SET 53

Food & Drink	1930s
Natural World	The Moon's gravitational pull
History	Shergar
Culture & Belief	Matthew
Stage & Screen	*Breakfast At Tiffany's*
Written Word	The Simpsons
Music	The Sex Pistols
Famous People	William Wallace and Robert the Bruce
Sport & Leisure	30
Science & Tech	35
True or False?	True

SET 54

Food & Drink	A Bath Oliver
Natural World	20 square feet
History	1801
Culture & Belief	The Salvation Army
Stage & Screen	The Simon Park Orchestra
Written Word	Homer
Music	*Cats*
Famous People	Jeremy Bentham
Sport & Leisure	Boston
Science & Tech	Four
True or False?	True

SET 55

Food & Drink	William Pitt the Younger
Natural World	Three (Scotland, Wales and England)
History	The *Queen Mary*, The *Queen Elizabeth* and *QEII*
Culture & Belief	The mini-skirt
Stage & Screen	Commander, Royal Navy

Written Word	James Joyce
Music	Abba's
Famous People	Matt Busby
Sport & Leisure	St Leger
Science & Tech	Strengthens it
True or False?	False (it was Chicago)

SET 56

Food & Drink	Tea
Natural World	Seven
History	Maundy Money
Culture & Belief	And the rest
Stage & Screen	Huey Lewis

Written Word	Percy Bysshe Shelley
Music	Scott Joplin
Famous People	Michael Flatley
Sport & Leisure	Baseball
Science & Tech	The elevator
True or False?	True

SET 57

Food & Drink	A tandoor (or clay oven)
Natural World	Scafell Pike
History	The privatisation of public assets
Culture & Belief	In the trunk
Stage & Screen	John Wayne
Written Word	Aristotle
Music	*Miss Saigon*
Famous People	Timothy Leary
Sport & Leisure	Epsom
Science & Tech	Vitamin C
True or False?	True

SET 58

Food & Drink	Fish and chips (they are salt and vinegar)
Natural World	Connacht, Ulster, Munster, Leinster
History	Texan Governor John Connolly
Culture & Belief	The Book of Revelation
Stage & Screen	*Some Like It Hot*
Written Word	Winston Churchill
Music	D'Oyly Carte
Famous People	Margaret Thatcher
Sport & Leisure	Baltimore
Science & Tech	Lime juice
True or False?	True

SET 59

Food & Drink	None (it's a fish)
Natural World	Belfast
History	The American railroad
Culture & Belief	Franz Hals
Stage & Screen	*Murder By Decree*
Written Word	*The Taming Of The Shrew*
Music	*Super Trooper*
Famous People	Mama Cass Elliot
Sport & Leisure	Augusta National Course, Georgia
Science & Tech	A rainbow
True or False?	False (it was William Olds)

SET 60

Food & Drink	In a distillery
Natural World	J. J. Audubon
History	The Crimean War
Culture & Belief	Your grace
Stage & Screen	Both were played by David Prowse
Written Word	Flashman
Music	Between two operatic scenes or acts
Famous People	John Lennon
Sport & Leisure	Cross-country skiing and rifle shooting
Science & Tech	Red and blue
True or False?	False

SET 61

Category	Answer
Food & Drink	Curry-flavoured soup
Natural World	Newly qualified doctors
History	Pudding Lane
Culture & Belief	25th March
Stage & Screen	*Ben Hur, Titanic, The Return of the King*
Written Word	Sancho Panza
Music	*My Favourite Things*
Famous People	Heather Locklear
Sport & Leisure	Three
Science & Tech	Hardness
True or False?	True

SET 62

Category	Answer
Food & Drink	The USA
Natural World	Oxygen and nitrogen
History	The League of Nations
Culture & Belief	The Royal Navy
Stage & Screen	Marlon Brando and Robert De Niro
Written Word	Domesday Book
Music	Amen Corner
Famous People	Ray Harryhausen
Sport & Leisure	Bowling
Science & Tech	Syphilis
True or False?	True

SET 63

Food & Drink	Bovril	Written Word	Dante Alighieri
Natural World	The South Pole	Music	A fever
History	Richard Nixon	Famous People	Richard Lester
Culture & Belief	Henry VIII	Sport & Leisure	Oxford
Stage & Screen	John Ford	Science & Tech	An apple falling on his head
		True or False?	False

SET 64

Food & Drink	Cocoa beans	Written Word	Anthony Burgess
Natural World	Penicillin	Music	Very loud
History	Eamon de Valera	Famous People	Emma Thompson
Culture & Belief	True love	Sport & Leisure	Joe Frasier and George Foreman
Stage & Screen	*A Clockwork Orange*	Science & Tech	'What You See Is What You Get'
		True or False?	True

SET 65

| Written Word | The Restaurant At The End Of The Universe |

| Food & Drink | An egg |

| Music | The Eagle |

| Natural World | Greenfly |

| Famous People | Clark Gable |

| History | Chaim Herzog |

| Sport & Leisure | 24 hours |

| Culture & Belief | 12 |

| Science & Tech | 88 |

| Stage & Screen | Oscar Hammerstein |

| True or False? | False |

SET 66

| Written Word | Robert Burns' |

| Food & Drink | Bows |

| Music | *My Old Man* |

| Natural World | Donegal |

| Famous People | Tommy Cooper's |

| History | Napoleon |

| Sport & Leisure | 64 |

| Culture & Belief | The *Argo* |

| Science & Tech | In the ear (it is 1 mm long) |

| Stage & Screen | *A Matter Of Life And Death* |

| True or False? | True |

SET 67

Food & Drink — It does not signify anything

Natural World — Ayers Rock

History — Dan Quayle

Culture & Belief — Faith, hope, charity, prudence, fortitude, justice, temperance

Stage & Screen — Sergio Leone

Written Word — Delilah

Music — When it is sung all the way through

Famous People — John F. Kennedy's

Sport & Leisure — Skiing

Science & Tech — Veteran

True or False? — False (it is a shrewdness)

SET 68

Food & Drink — Thanksgiving

Natural World — Nectar and pollen

History — 116 years (1337–1453)

Culture & Belief — Pride, gluttony, lust, anger, sloth, envy, covetousness

Stage & Screen — *High Noon*

Written Word — He was staked through the heart and beheaded

Music — Country & Western

Famous People — Sid Vicious

Sport & Leisure — England and Australia

Science & Tech — Another diamond

True or False? — False (Britain has no written constitution)

SET 69

Written Word	*Whisky Galore*
Food & Drink	Tonic water
Music	Vince Hill
Natural World	The albatross (4 m)
Famous People	Fatty Arbuckle
History	H. H. Kitchener
Sport & Leisure	Jimmy White
Culture & Belief	8 days
Science & Tech	Lies
Stage & Screen	*Escape To Victory*
True or False?	False

SET 70

Written Word	*Kidnapped* and *Catriona*
Food & Drink	The first is Scotch; the other isn't
Music	Keep the red flag flying here
Natural World	The peregrine (112 mph)
Famous People	Phil Spector
History	The Napoleonic Wars
Sport & Leisure	Gary Sobers
Culture & Belief	Pentecost
Science & Tech	24
Stage & Screen	*The Quiet Man*
True or False?	False (it was Mr Goodyear)

SET 71

Food & Drink	432
Natural World	Bread
History	King Edward I
Culture & Belief	1,788
Stage & Screen	Wimbledon Common
Written Word	The Arabian Nights Entertainment
Music	The book of the performance
Famous People	Elvis Costello
Sport & Leisure	Korea
Science & Tech	30 stone
True or False?	True

SET 72

Food & Drink	William Kellogg
Natural World	Burma
History	Four
Culture & Belief	Vietnam
Stage & Screen	*The Poseidon Adventure*
Written Word	The Dead Sea Scrolls
Music	Julio Iglesias
Famous People	33
Sport & Leisure	Kayak and Canadian
Science & Tech	Away from it
True or False?	False (fire needs air to burn)

SET 73

Food & Drink
The Earl of Sandwich

Natural World
The North Sea and the Baltic

History
It was stolen from Westminster Abbey

Culture & Belief
Red

Stage & Screen
Rear Window

Written Word
Knitting

Music
Dolly Parton and Whitney Houston

Famous People
Adolf Hitler

Sport & Leisure
French & Australian championships, US Open, Wimbledon

Science & Tech
In the air

True or False?
True

SET 74

Food & Drink
A herring

Natural World
It has no tail

History
Israel beat Egypt, Jordan and Syria

Culture & Belief
Mancunium

Stage & Screen
It's A Wonderful Life

Written Word
Mrs Rochester

Music
Line dancing

Famous People
Anna Pavlova

Sport & Leisure
Russia

Science & Tech
Adrenalin

True or False?
True

SET 75

Food & Drink	Caviare
Natural World	Beijing
History	Henri IV
Culture & Belief	Beijing
Stage & Screen	Paul Michael Glaser

Written Word	Mrs Hudson
Music	Billy Ray Cyrus
Famous People	Frank Sinatra
Sport & Leisure	England
Science & Tech	In the sky (they are constellations)
True or False?	False (it is an architectural feature)

SET 76

Food & Drink	George Bush
Natural World	Turkey
History	1840
Culture & Belief	Mandarin
Stage & Screen	*Robocop*

Written Word	*Wind In The Willows*
Music	Jerusalem
Famous People	Charles II
Sport & Leisure	1971
Science & Tech	The body's vital organs
True or False?	True

SET 77

Food & Drink	German beer
Natural World	Four
History	The Beatles
Culture & Belief	2(10 + 4 − 12)
Stage & Screen	Marlon Brando
Written Word	Rip Van Winkle
Music	The piccolo
Famous People	Piracy
Sport & Leisure	Yellow, red, black, blue, green
Science & Tech	Laser
True or False?	False (it has 22)

SET 78

Food & Drink	On a chicken
Natural World	A boy
History	The 16th century
Culture & Belief	A bench
Stage & Screen	Walter, John and Angelica Huston
Written Word	Robert Graves
Music	Noël Coward
Famous People	7
Sport & Leisure	Kent and Surrey
Science & Tech	Lines of latitude
True or False?	True

SET 79

Food & Drink	Apples
Natural World	Tokyo
History	The Bastille prison
Culture & Belief	Matthias
Stage & Screen	*Up Pompeii*
Written Word	*Casino Royale*
Music	Steve Earle
Famous People	Prince and Madonna
Sport & Leisure	Manchester City
Science & Tech	William Huskisson MP, Trade Secretary
True or False?	False (3 are)

SET 80

Food & Drink	Heineken
Natural World	Moscow
History	Tiananmen Square
Culture & Belief	Religion
Stage & Screen	Yosser Hughes (in *Boys From The Blackstuff*)
Written Word	*Animal Farm*
Music	*HMS Pinafore*
Famous People	Bruce Springsteen
Sport & Leisure	It was the first women's cricket club
Science & Tech	13 (they are prime numbers)
True or False?	False

SET 81

Food & Drink	Kosher food
Natural World	Coal
History	1793
Culture & Belief	The
Stage & Screen	Terry Gilliam

Written Word	F. Scott Fitzgerald
Music	*Young Love*
Famous People	Shirley Temple
Sport & Leisure	Martin Peters and Geoff Hurst (3)
Science & Tech	Uranus
True or False?	False

SET 82

Food & Drink	Pancakes
Natural World	The Mariana Trench
History	The eighth century
Culture & Belief	A fresco
Stage & Screen	He is assistant to the senior electrician

Written Word	Banquo's
Music	Bill Clinton
Famous People	The Duke of York
Sport & Leisure	Curling
Science & Tech	A rainbow
True or False?	False (it is a type of lake)

SET 83

Food & Drink	Bicarbonate of soda	Written Word	Guinevere
Natural World	Light Equatorial winds	Music	John McCormack
History	Charles II	Famous People	Samuel Morse
Culture & Belief	A type of pottery	Sport & Leisure	Stanley Matthews
Stage & Screen	*The Towering Inferno*	Science & Tech	6th century BC (in Rome)
		True or False?	False (it was a fake)

SET 84

Food & Drink	Bordeaux	Written Word	Lilliput
Natural World	Elbrus	Music	Kurt Weill and Bertolt Brecht
History	Prohibition on alcohol sales began	Famous People	Ronald Reagan
Culture & Belief	Ballet dancing	Sport & Leisure	1903
Stage & Screen	Velma	Science & Tech	Six
		True or False?	False (it is closely related to raccoons)

SET 85

| | | Written Word | Pygmalion |

| Food & Drink | The geese | Music | Chicory Tip |

| Natural World | Smallpox | Famous People | American |

| History | Ireland and Denmark | Sport & Leisure | 6 |

| Culture & Belief | 6th January (Feast of the Three Kings) | Science & Tech | The Southern Cross |

| Stage & Screen | Chuck Jones | True or False? | True |

SET 86

| | | Written Word | Huckleberry Finn |

| Food & Drink | Carbon dioxide | Music | Napoleon's retreat from Moscow |

| Natural World | Captain Scott's South Pole voyage | Famous People | Rhodesia (now Zimbabwe) |

| History | Britain's first flushing public toilets opened on Fleet St | Sport & Leisure | A championship belt |

| Culture & Belief | Jesuits | Science & Tech | 1820s |

| Stage & Screen | 'Cubby' Broccoli produced the Bond movies | True or False? | True |

SET 87

(Food & Drink) Orange

(Natural World) A deadly toadstool

(History) Catholicism

(Culture & Belief) Australian Aborigines

(Stage & Screen) *Rocky*

(Written Word) *The Pied Piper of Hamelin*

(Music) Chuck Berry

(Famous People) Edmund Hillary

(Sport & Leisure) The Whitbread Round The World Yacht Race

(Science & Tech) From its first six letter keys

(True or False?) True

SET 88

(Food & Drink) Haricot beans

(Natural World) The dog

(History) Maroon

(Culture & Belief) The first five books of the Bible

(Stage & Screen) Jacques Tati

(Written Word) King Lear

(Music) Henry VIII

(Famous People) Ian Paisley

(Sport & Leisure) Greyhounds

(Science & Tech) On the Moon

(True or False?) False (it is a Russian horse)

SET 89

Food & Drink	A thickener
Natural World	The adder
History	Winston Churchill
Culture & Belief	Arches
Stage & Screen	*La Dolce Vita*

Written Word	*Lady Chatterley's Lover*
Music	Buddy Holly
Famous People	Charles Blondin
Sport & Leisure	'Empty hand'
Science & Tech	Venus'
True or False?	True

SET 90

Food & Drink	Sugar
Natural World	Insects
History	Winston Churchill
Culture & Belief	They had live snakes for hair
Stage & Screen	*The Seven Samurai*

Written Word	Carson McCullers
Music	*Hansel And Gretel*
Famous People	Aleister Crowley
Sport & Leisure	Asymmetrical bars, beam, horse-vault, floor exercises
Science & Tech	Poisons
True or False?	False (they have the same colours, but reversed)

SET 91

Food & Drink	Monosodium glutamate
Natural World	The 17th century
History	Winston Churchill
Culture & Belief	The Coca-Cola bottle
Stage & Screen	*The Seventh Seal*

Written Word	*Midnight's Children*
Music	Roy 'C'
Famous People	Lloyd George
Sport & Leisure	Ireland
Science & Tech	Light waves
True or False?	False (bats can fly)

SET 92

Food & Drink	It is fed by workers to queen bees
Natural World	5 litres (8 pints)
History	Gerald Ford
Culture & Belief	Admiral of the Fleet
Stage & Screen	Jake La Motta

Written Word	Percy Bysshe Shelley
Music	*Minnie The Moocher*
Famous People	El Greco
Sport & Leisure	Hockey
Science & Tech	Sputnik 1
True or False?	True

SET 93

Food & Drink	Rum
Natural World	Off Australia's north-east coast
History	The Community Charge
Culture & Belief	Art Deco
Stage & Screen	*The Terminator*
Written Word	Quasimodo
Music	Bob Dylan
Famous People	Victoria
Sport & Leisure	Wrestling
Science & Tech	Cancers in the human body
True or False?	True

SET 94

Food & Drink	Plums
Natural World	The speed of its wings beating
History	Seven
Culture & Belief	The London Underground map
Stage & Screen	Ars Gratia Artis
Written Word	*The Daily Planet*
Music	*Land Of Hope And Glory*
Famous People	Herod the Great
Sport & Leisure	Ice Hockey
Science & Tech	Voyager 2
True or False?	False

SET 95

Written Word			Edgar Allan Poe
Food & Drink	Peach Melba (after Nellie Melba)	Music	Harry Chapin
Natural World	The Galapagos Islands	Famous People	Billie Holiday
History	Mikhail Gorbachev	Sport & Leisure	Italy
Culture & Belief	The USSR	Science & Tech	Wind speed
Stage & Screen	Jack Wild	True or False?	False (it was the House of Lords)

SET 96

Written Word			The Drones
Food & Drink	Changed water into wine	Music	The exciseman
Natural World	46	Famous People	The Morris Mini
History	Edward Heath	Sport & Leisure	15
Culture & Belief	Diapers	Science & Tech	Halley's Comet
Stage & Screen	*Creature Comforts, A Close Shave, The Wrong Trousers*	True or False?	False (it was the Morris Minor)

SET 97

Food & Drink	Veal
Natural World	Hippopotamus
History	They were father and daughter
Culture & Belief	Stirling
Stage & Screen	Richard Chamberlain
Written Word	*The Gulag Archipelago*
Music	Johann Strauss I and II
Famous People	Fitzgerald
Sport & Leisure	12th dan
Science & Tech	Apollo 10 (at 39,897 kph)
True or False?	False (it is the biggest)

SET 98

Food & Drink	5000
Natural World	Six metres
History	Nelson Mandela
Culture & Belief	Brigham Young
Stage & Screen	*Oklahoma!*
Written Word	Graham Greene
Music	Elvis Costello
Famous People	Oscar Wilde and Charles Stewart Parnell
Sport & Leisure	Fencing
Science & Tech	Fool's gold
True or False?	True

SET 99

Food & Drink	Simnel cake
Natural World	A yard
History	Oxford
Culture & Belief	Two
Stage & Screen	The Nazi party
Written Word	London
Music	Benny Goodman
Famous People	Erwin Rommel
Sport & Leisure	A crosse
Science & Tech	60 ft
True or False?	True

SET 100

Food & Drink	Types of coffee
Natural World	Talc
History	President Franklin D. Roosevelt
Culture & Belief	The front (or bow)
Stage & Screen	The Twilight Zone
Written Word	Athos, Porthos and Aramis
Music	The Old Triangle
Famous People	Muhammad Ali
Sport & Leisure	The Daily Express
Science & Tech	Chlorophyll
True or False?	False (it is an insect which eats book bindings)

SET 101

Food & Drink	Tea leaves
Natural World	Carboniferous
History	Beefeaters
Culture & Belief	A tent-maker
Stage & Screen	Larry Hagman

Written Word	By setting all the action in *Ulysses* on that day
Music	*Hoots Mon*
Famous People	The Duke of York
Sport & Leisure	Kenny Dalgliesh
Science & Tech	Apollo 11
True or False?	False

SET 102

Food & Drink	Sausages baked in batter
Natural World	23½ degrees
History	All were British prime ministers
Culture & Belief	Canterbury
Stage & Screen	Southfork

Written Word	Bull's-Eye
Music	Alan Freed
Famous People	Princess Grace (Grace Kelly)
Sport & Leisure	Croquet
Science & Tech	TNT
True or False?	False (Indira Gandhi held office longer over two terms)

SET 103

| Food & Drink | Figs |

| Written Word | Phileas Fogg and Passepartout |

| Music | The holly |

| Natural World | 760 mph (1200 kph) |

| Famous People | They were the original Siamese twins |

| History | Robert the Bruce |

| Sport & Leisure | 7 |

| Culture & Belief | Amerigo Vespucci |

| Science & Tech | Nuclear fission |

| Stage & Screen | Jersey |

| True or False? | True |

SET 104

| Written Word | Winnie-the-Pooh |

| Food & Drink | Shortbread, caramel and chocolate |

| Music | *Eve Of Destruction* |

| Natural World | His brain |

| Famous People | David Cassidy |

| History | To defeat the Romans in battle |

| Sport & Leisure | Softball |

| Culture & Belief | China |

| Science & Tech | Nickel |

| Stage & Screen | Penelope Keith |

| True or False? | False (it was Jimmy Saville) |

SET 105

Food & Drink	Fried onion and potato cakes
Natural World	Galileo
History	Sir Francis Drake
Culture & Belief	505 (5 + 500)
Stage & Screen	*Hi-De-Hi*

Written Word	A cynic
Music	David Bowie's
Famous People	Alexander Dubcek
Sport & Leisure	Long-distance cycling, swimming and running
Science & Tech	The mercury used in hat manufacture
True or False?	True

SET 106

Food & Drink	There is no legal definition
Natural World	Its 3630 m altitude lacks the oxygen to sustain a large fire
History	The Boston Tea Party
Culture & Belief	Athens
Stage & Screen	Bruce Willis

Written Word	Mellors (the gamekeeper)
Music	Edith Piaf
Famous People	Lord Haw-Haw
Sport & Leisure	Celtic
Science & Tech	The square root of a negative number
True or False?	False (it was his brother, Rezin; Jim only popularised it)

SET 107

Food & Drink — Orange

Natural World — Horses

History — 1620

Culture & Belief — Cock-a-doodle-doo

Stage & Screen — Derek Jacobi

Written Word — Silver bells, cockle shells and pretty maids all in a row

Music — Led Zeppelin

Famous People — Lord Louis Mountbatten

Sport & Leisure — Thailand

Science & Tech — An albino

True or False? — True (in 1880)

SET 108

Food & Drink — Almond-flavoured paste (for cakes)

Natural World — Francis of Assisi

History — Charles de Gaulle

Culture & Belief — 11

Stage & Screen — *Neighbours*

Written Word — Arthur Dent

Music — Aretha Franklin

Famous People — Count Dracula

Sport & Leisure — The Crucible Theatre, Sheffield

Science & Tech — Turn base metals into gold

True or False? — False (At 43, Teddy Roosevelt was a year younger)

SET 109

Food & Drink	Mexico
Natural World	Atlantis
History	Clement Attlee
Culture & Belief	Albert Einstein
Stage & Screen	All were written by Ben Elton

Written Word	Niccolò Machiavelli
Music	The Ramones
Famous People	Paul VI, John Paul I and John Paul II
Sport & Leisure	Arsenal
Science & Tech	Neutrons
True or False?	False (it is O positive)

SET 110

Food & Drink	Green
Natural World	It performs no function
History	The Liberals
Culture & Belief	Jacob
Stage & Screen	*The Waltons*

Written Word	The sinking of the Argentinian battleship *Belgrano*
Music	A young cowboy all wrapped in white linen
Famous People	Geoffrey Howe
Sport & Leisure	Shinty
Science & Tech	Ozone
True or False?	True (on 14th January 1878)

SET 111

Food & Drink	Pig-offal loaf
Natural World	Frogs, gnats, flies, locusts
History	The IRA launched a mortar attack on the building
Culture & Belief	All are originally Indian words
Stage & Screen	Steven Spielberg
Written Word	Anne Of Green Gables
Music	The Ugly Bugs' Ball
Famous People	Mae West
Sport & Leisure	5 (France, Holland, Belgium, Italy, Spain)
Science & Tech	1024
True or False?	False (it was Johannes Gutenberg)

SET 112

Food & Drink	Avocados
Natural World	A cock crowing
History	1934
Culture & Belief	Walk along it
Stage & Screen	To synchronise sound and action in a scene
Written Word	The 1983 Labour Party election manifesto
Music	Buddy Holly and The Crickets
Famous People	Rudolf Hess
Sport & Leisure	The Fairs Cup
Science & Tech	A headache (it is aspirin)
True or False?	True

SET 113

Food & Drink	Gruel
Natural World	Lizard Point, Cornwall
History	He shot President Reagan
Culture & Belief	Farm equipment
Stage & Screen	Jess
Written Word	Lord Byron
Music	Paul McCartney
Famous People	The Wellington (he was the duke)
Sport & Leisure	Dark blue
Science & Tech	The pancreas
True or False?	True

SET 114

Food & Drink	Vodka
Natural World	Loch Lomond
History	The pilots who fought the Battle of Britain
Culture & Belief	Confucius
Stage & Screen	Ringo Starr
Written Word	John Knox
Music	Detroit, Michigan
Famous People	To mark the death of Henry Royce
Sport & Leisure	The European Champion Clubs' Cup
Science & Tech	Cats' eyes
True or False?	True

SET 115

Food & Drink	Sweetcorn
Natural World	The tortoise (at 80+ years)
History	1988
Culture & Belief	The Guides
Stage & Screen	Basil Fawlty
Written Word	Gabriel Garcia Marquez
Music	Motor Town (Detroit is a major car-production centre)
Famous People	Frank Sinatra
Sport & Leisure	Green, yellow and white with red polka dots
Science & Tech	The Channel Tunnel
True or False?	True

SET 116

Food & Drink	Cauliflower
Natural World	The duck-billed platypus
History	Harold Wilson
Culture & Belief	Avalon
Stage & Screen	Jim Henson
Written Word	George Orwell
Music	John Williams
Famous People	Al Jolson
Sport & Leisure	Extreme fatigue (it's the cyclists' 'pain barrier')
Science & Tech	Carbon Dioxide
True or False?	False (they were the government)

SET 117

Written Word	Moriarty		

Food & Drink	Ice-cream	Music	Trombone

Natural World	Swifts	Famous People	Charlie Chaplin's

History	The Great Plague	Sport & Leisure	Winks

Culture & Belief	Paul	Science & Tech	The amount of space it occupies on a surface

Stage & Screen	*Saturday Night Live*	True or False?	False (it is a fish)

SET 118

Written Word	The Reichenbach Falls		

Food & Drink	It is the start of the grouse-shooting season	Music	Eric Idle

Natural World	3 for different functions (Bloemfontein, Cape Town, Pretoria)	Famous People	Guy Gibson

History	Finland	Sport & Leisure	Munro-bagging (climbing mountains over 3000 ft)

Culture & Belief	St George, St Andrew, St Patrick	Science & Tech	On a church (they are parts of the building)

Stage & Screen	Bill and Ben	True or False?	False

SET 119

Food & Drink	Tiramisù
Natural World	Jordan
History	Cut off part of his ear
Culture & Belief	Nirvana
Stage & Screen	Martin and Gary Kemp
Written Word	Samuel Pepys
Music	Andrew Ridgeley
Famous People	Kurt Cobain
Sport & Leisure	Christopher Chataway
Science & Tech	Architectural columns
True or False?	True

SET 120

Food & Drink	A waiter (it is a tip)
Natural World	Highland Region
History	Mexico
Culture & Belief	The infectious diarrhoea suffered by tourists in Mexico
Stage & Screen	John Belushi and Dan Aykroyd
Written Word	Adolf Hitler
Music	Will Powers
Famous People	Jean Shrimpton
Sport & Leisure	Gareth Southgate
Science & Tech	20
True or False?	False; it is a set of bells hung in a tower

SET 121

Food & Drink	Drambuie
Natural World	Armenia
History	11
Culture & Belief	Honey bees
Stage & Screen	Tinky Winky
Written Word	The Thompson Twins
Music	There were three of them
Famous People	John Gummer
Sport & Leisure	Darts
Science & Tech	Meccano
True or False?	True

SET 122

Food & Drink	Russia
Natural World	Earthworm
History	England's medieval wealth from wool
Culture & Belief	The Lord Chancellor
Stage & Screen	Dipsy
Written Word	Tin Tin's
Music	Cherry pink and apple blossom white
Famous People	Carrots
Sport & Leisure	Brown
Science & Tech	Brown
True or False?	True

SET 123

Food & Drink — 7lbs (3.2kg)

Natural World — Kent

History — Madrid

Culture & Belief — Madrid

Stage & Screen — *Due South*

Written Word — The cruellest month

Music — Fats

Famous People — Canterbury Cathedral

Sport & Leisure — Seven

Science & Tech — The earth

True or False? — False (it was Wilkie Collins)

SET 124

Food & Drink — Ten

Natural World — Both male and female

History — Buttons at the cuff

Culture & Belief — St Paul's

Stage & Screen — $250,000

Written Word — Sherlock Holmes

Music — Maurice (by one hour)

Famous People — The Nation of Islam

Sport & Leisure — Elephant

Science & Tech — Red, yellow, blue

True or False? — False

SET 125

Food & Drink	Potato
Natural World	Central Park
History	Minister of Propaganda
Culture & Belief	Right
Stage & Screen	Homer, Marge, Bart, Lisa, Maggie
Written Word	One day it'll keep you
Music	*Whole Lotta Love*
Famous People	Victor Emmanuel II
Sport & Leisure	5 feet
Science & Tech	Three (red, green, blue)
True or False?	False (red, yellow and blue)

SET 126

Food & Drink	Soya-bean curd
Natural World	New York (Central Park)
History	Lady Godiva
Culture & Belief	A book
Stage & Screen	Smithers
Written Word	Albert Einstein
Music	Led Zeppelin
Famous People	11th
Sport & Leisure	Tug-of-war
Science & Tech	Cast iron
True or False?	False

SET 127

Food & Drink	Mushrooms

Natural World	20 sq ft

History	Two

Culture & Belief	Faith, hope and charity

Stage & Screen	Jane Russell

Written Word	Brunettes

Music	James

Famous People	36

Sport & Leisure	One

Science & Tech	Dolly (the sheep)

True or False?	False (it was the Tornados' *Telstar*)

SET 128

Food & Drink	Stuff a mushroom

Natural World	12

History	Catherine

Culture & Belief	East of Eden

Stage & Screen	Jaclyn Smith, Kate Jackson, Farrah Fawcett (-Majors)

Written Word	Cain

Music	*Lucy in the Sky with Diamonds*

Famous People	George Harrison

Sport & Leisure	London

Science & Tech	Pi (π)

True or False?	True

SET 129

Food & Drink	Dried insects
Natural World	The mosquito
History	Two
Culture & Belief	12
Stage & Screen	The Goons
Written Word	Beelzebub
Music	The Rolling Stones
Famous People	Francis Chichester
Sport & Leisure	He ran the race barefoot
Science & Tech	3.14 or $^{22}/_{7}$
True or False?	True

SET 130

Food & Drink	4
Natural World	X
History	Brother-in-law
Culture & Belief	Thor
Stage & Screen	Anakin Skywalker
Written Word	*Blade Runner*
Music	Frank Sinatra
Famous People	Bing Crosby
Sport & Leisure	Zola Budd
Science & Tech	Celsius
True or False?	True

SET 131

Food & Drink	Bromine
Natural World	23
History	A wall-hanging
Culture & Belief	Transport & General Workers' Union
Stage & Screen	Borsetshire
Written Word	Hamlet
Music	Siobhan Fahey was a member of both
Famous People	Frank Sinatra
Sport & Leisure	Ian Botham
Science & Tech	Belfast
True or False?	False (it is Falstaff)

SET 132

Food & Drink	Trifle
Natural World	Tunisia
History	It was awarded to Malta in 1942
Culture & Belief	The George Cross
Stage & Screen	Humphrey Bogart
Written Word	A hedgehog
Music	The paintings on your wall
Famous People	Orson Welles
Sport & Leisure	The Marathon
Science & Tech	Blackpool
True or False?	True

SET 133

Food & Drink	Soup
Natural World	The iris
History	24
Culture & Belief	Good of themselves
Stage & Screen	*The Third Man*

Written Word	A troll
Music	A wooden chair
Famous People	William Randolph Hearst
Sport & Leisure	One
Science & Tech	365 ft
True or False?	False

SET 134

Food & Drink	Mayonnaise
Natural World	Lion and tiger
History	10
Culture & Belief	Love
Stage & Screen	Honor Blackman

Written Word	Christopher Robin
Music	Eternal
Famous People	Aubrey Beardsley
Sport & Leisure	Rangers
Science & Tech	Cantilever
True or False?	True

SET 135

| Written Word | The Water Margin |

| Food & Drink | Water |

| Music | 7 swans a-swimming |

| Natural World | 120 in (300 cm) |

| Famous People | William Wordsworth |

| History | 4 |

| Sport & Leisure | Synchronised swimming |

| Culture & Belief | Cancer, Scorpio and Pisces |

| Science & Tech | Water |

| Stage & Screen | Mrs Goggins |

| True or False? | True |

SET 136

| Written Word | Robert Burns |

| Food & Drink | Flaky |

| Music | Viva España |

| Natural World | Daddy-longlegs |

| Famous People | Two |

| History | William the Conqueror |

| Sport & Leisure | Manchester |

| Culture & Belief | Vesta |

| Science & Tech | Greenwich Observatory |

| Stage & Screen | Steve Coogan |

| True or False? | False |

SET 137

Food & Drink	Thousand leaves
Natural World	12,000 miles
History	Harold Macmillan
Culture & Belief	Lancelot
Stage & Screen	Sam Peckinpah
Written Word	The cheque book
Music	Anni-Frid (Frida)
Famous People	He was an MP
Sport & Leisure	Cards
Science & Tech	Roger Penrose
True or False?	True

SET 138

Food & Drink	Stilton
Natural World	Avebury
History	The Hole in the Wall Gang
Culture & Belief	*The Angel of the North*
Stage & Screen	*Butch Cassidy and the Sundance Kid*
Written Word	He was already married
Music	*The Marseillaise*
Famous People	Maria Callas
Sport & Leisure	Marco Pantani
Science & Tech	The Michelin Man
True or False?	False

SET 139

Written Word		George Bernard Shaw wrote it
Food & Drink	Bacteria	Music	Van Morrison
Natural World	The Dominican Republic & Haiti	Famous People	Noël Coward
History	Haiti	Sport & Leisure	British Open, US Open, US Masters, US PGA
Culture & Belief	The first harvest of the first settlers	Science & Tech	Different colours
Stage & Screen	Perdita or Pongo	True or False?	False

SET 140

Written Word		Big Brother
Food & Drink	Preserved beef on rye bread	Music	*That's Amore*
Natural World	The moon	Famous People	Gene Roddenberry and Timothy Leary
History	USSR	Sport & Leisure	Three
Culture & Belief	Guru Nanak	Science & Tech	Nine
Stage & Screen	Pluto	True or False?	False (she appeared in the original series)

SET 141

| Written Word | Leslie Halliwell |

| Food & Drink | Green |

| Music | Mike McGear |

| Natural World | The Shetland Islands |

| Famous People | Michael Fagin |

| History | The NHS |

| Sport & Leisure | Canada |

| Culture & Belief | The crucifixion of Christ |

| Science & Tech | Harris tweed |

| Stage & Screen | Ron Moody |

| True or False? | False (it is the Falabella) |

SET 142

| Written Word | Long John Silver |

| Food & Drink | Bicarbonate of soda |

| Music | The Scaffold |

| Natural World | 32 |

| Famous People | Samoa |

| History | It brought the first West Indian immigrants |

| Sport & Leisure | 1968 |

| Culture & Belief | Easter |

| Science & Tech | Four |

| Stage & Screen | Toothpaste |

| True or False? | True |

SET 143

Food & Drink	Ministry of Agriculture, Fisheries & Food
Natural World	The USA
History	1776
Culture & Belief	Go to sleep (it's a sleeping pill)
Stage & Screen	Kojak
Written Word	He had a lean and hungry look
Music	Ginger Baker, Jack Bruce, Eric Clapton
Famous People	Twiggy
Sport & Leisure	8 stones
Science & Tech	Four
True or False?	False

SET 144

Food & Drink	Tea
Natural World	Vermont
History	America won independence in 1776
Culture & Belief	Samaritan
Stage & Screen	*The Likely Lads* and *Whatever Happened to the Likely Lads?*
Written Word	Captain Flint
Music	*Tubular Bells* by Mike Oldfield
Famous People	America (the continent)
Sport & Leisure	Every three years
Science & Tech	UK (in 1936, three years before the USA)
True or False?	True

SET 145

| Food & Drink | Pineapple |

| Natural World | Breastbone |

| History | George Washington |

| Culture & Belief | Killing the hydra |

| Stage & Screen | Gerald Scarfe |

| Written Word | House-For-One |

| Music | Ray and Dave Davies |

| Famous People | Gerald Scarfe |

| Sport & Leisure | Joe Davis |

| Science & Tech | Collar bone |

| True or False? | False |

SET 146

| Food & Drink | Both are soups, served cold |

| Natural World | Paradoxical or REM |

| History | Carnaby Street |

| Culture & Belief | 13 |

| Stage & Screen | Clint Eastwood |

| Written Word | *A Tale of Two Cities* |

| Music | *Cockles & Mussels, Alive, Alive-O* |

| Famous People | Jeremy Irons |

| Sport & Leisure | Brazil |

| Science & Tech | She was the first woman in space |

| True or False? | True |

SET 147

Food & Drink	Red wine
Natural World	Rapid Eye Movement
History	He was the first PM to be assassinated
Culture & Belief	Buddhism
Stage & Screen	Fr Jack

Written Word	Left (*My Left Foot*)
Music	The Labour Party
Famous People	Robin Cook
Sport & Leisure	7
Science & Tech	28
True or False?	False

SET 148

Food & Drink	Brandy
Natural World	They carry and suckle their young in body pouches
History	Pompeii
Culture & Belief	Pub signs (outdoor)
Stage & Screen	*The X-Files*

Written Word	Mr Sparks
Music	Al (*You Can Call Me Al*)
Famous People	Journalist
Sport & Leisure	Scotland
Science & Tech	14
True or False?	False (it is 'Q')

SET 149

Food & Drink	Roughage
Natural World	An albatross
History	Cigarette advertising
Culture & Belief	No
Stage & Screen	Ross and Monica
Written Word	He is a taxi-driver
Music	It was their 1st non-Beatles US no 1
Famous People	The Beatles
Sport & Leisure	A raised deck at a ship's rear
Science & Tech	Liver
True or False?	False (it's women's fragrances)

SET 150

Food & Drink	None
Natural World	Yellow
History	She was the first woman elected MP
Culture & Belief	Beautiful women
Stage & Screen	Bond girls
Written Word	Dr No
Music	Men at Work
Famous People	Bob Holness
Sport & Leisure	A catamaran
Science & Tech	Gold
True or False?	True

SET 151

Food & Drink	C
Natural World	4500
History	Before the American Civil War
Culture & Belief	Nicene, Apostles and Athanasian
Stage & Screen	*Listen With Mother*

Written Word	A Babylonian King
Music	Jimmy Young
Famous People	John Adams
Sport & Leisure	On *Gladiators* TV show
Science & Tech	1kg
True or False?	True

SET 152

Food & Drink	Fat
Natural World	Oxford
History	The Nazi Party
Culture & Belief	Diana
Stage & Screen	Pluto

Written Word	1931
Music	The Sex Pistols
Famous People	John Smith
Sport & Leisure	Hammersmith and Barnes
Science & Tech	1868
True or False?	True

SET 153

		Written Word	Jack Kerouac
Food & Drink	Yeast extract	Music	A coolabah tree
Natural World	A troop	Famous People	William Wilberforce
History	Knight of the Thistle	Sport & Leisure	Goolagong
Culture & Belief	Paddle in it	Science & Tech	Amsterdam
Stage & Screen	The name shows the film's director disowned it	True or False?	True

SET 154

		Written Word	All the perfumes of Arabia
Food & Drink	Atlanta, Georgia	Music	Waylon Jennings
Natural World	The Canaries	Famous People	Pope
History	Macbeth	Sport & Leisure	Foil
Culture & Belief	East Timor	Science & Tech	Jupiter
Stage & Screen	A Volkswagen Beetle	True or False?	True

SET 155

Food & Drink	Dyspepsia (indigestion)
Natural World	Indigestion
History	Nelson
Culture & Belief	I think, therefore I am
Stage & Screen	Alan Ladd (in *Shane*)
Written Word	Open sesame
Music	John Lennon
Famous People	Warren Beatty (her brother)
Sport & Leisure	He is left-handed
Science & Tech	18
True or False?	True

SET 156

Food & Drink	Homepride
Natural World	Crocus
History	The Gregorian calendar
Culture & Belief	August
Stage & Screen	*The Pit and the Pendulum*
Written Word	Ali Baba
Music	*You Never Can Tell*
Famous People	Sharon Stone
Sport & Leisure	Bobby Jones
Science & Tech	180°
True or False?	True (it lasted 115 years)

SET 157

Category	Answer
Food & Drink	Honey
Natural World	A cete
History	Edward II
Culture & Belief	Christmas
Stage & Screen	Callahan
Written Word	Isaac Asimov
Music	Flodden
Famous People	Buddhism
Sport & Leisure	0-0
Science & Tech	Halley's Comet
True or False?	False (it would be quick and lively)

SET 158

Category	Answer
Food & Drink	20
Natural World	K2
History	Wat Tyler
Culture & Belief	Abraham
Stage & Screen	They all subsequently became sitcoms
Written Word	Emily
Music	Tchaikovsky
Famous People	Richard Gere and Cindy Crawford
Sport & Leisure	It's higher in the centre
Science & Tech	75 years
True or False?	False

SET 159

Food & Drink	Basil
Natural World	The Tropic of Cancer (23½°N)
History	Richard II
Culture & Belief	Virgo
Stage & Screen	FAB 1

Written Word	Melvyn Bragg
Music	*Pathetique*
Famous People	Bill Gates
Sport & Leisure	An angler (these are knots)
Science & Tech	Disk operating system
True or False?	False (it was Ararat)

SET 160

Food & Drink	Wheat flour
Natural World	A fish
History	Jack the Ripper
Culture & Belief	Death
Stage & Screen	Frank Oz (he operated both)

Written Word	In a horse-riding accident
Music	Marc Bolan and Bing Crosby
Famous People	He played himself
Sport & Leisure	Muhammad Ali
Science & Tech	Star Wars
True or False?	False (it was England)

SET 161

Food & Drink	Fruits or seeds
Natural World	Captain Cook
History	Korea
Culture & Belief	The Magic Circle
Stage & Screen	The Banana Splits
Written Word	Julian Barnes
Music	*Spiceworld – The Movie*
Famous People	Nelson Mandela and F. W. de Klerk
Sport & Leisure	England and Australia
Science & Tech	Three hours
True or False?	False

SET 162

Food & Drink	Cereal (Ceres)
Natural World	The Sandwich Isles
History	Roy Jenkins and William Rodgers
Culture & Belief	Apollo
Stage & Screen	*Groundhog Day*
Written Word	Molesworth
Music	KC and the Sunshine Band
Famous People	Damien Hirst
Sport & Leisure	The museum at Lord's
Science & Tech	Gabriel Fahrenheit
True or False?	True

SET 163

Food & Drink	Salt
Natural World	Alaska
History	Henry Pu-Yi
Culture & Belief	*Zeitgeist*
Stage & Screen	Baldrick
Written Word	24
Music	Dora Bryan
Famous People	Queen Mary
Sport & Leisure	Franz Beckenbauer
Science & Tech	Panama Canal
True or False?	True

SET 164

Food & Drink	A bat
Natural World	Dover, Hastings, Hythe, Romney and Sandwich
History	Emmeline Pankhurst
Culture & Belief	The emperor of Japan
Stage & Screen	The *Carry On* films
Written Word	Thomas the Tank Engine
Music	Gilbert and Sullivan
Famous People	Ceylon
Sport & Leisure	Surfing
Science & Tech	The Mercedes Benz car
True or False?	False

SET 165

Food & Drink	Pasteurisation
Natural World	Brindisi
History	Corazon Aquino
Culture & Belief	On a baby's bottom
Stage & Screen	The *Carry On* films
Written Word	Sodor
Music	Neil Innes
Famous People	Literature
Sport & Leisure	Croquet
Science & Tech	Pierre and Marie Curie
True or False?	True

SET 166

Food & Drink	A dried plum
Natural World	Pearl Harbour
History	The Brownie
Culture & Belief	Your car would have had a minor shunt
Stage & Screen	*Carry on … Up The Khyber*
Written Word	Charlie Chaplin
Music	*A Hard Day's Night*
Famous People	Jimmy Saville
Sport & Leisure	Surfing
Science & Tech	Sony and Philips
True or False?	False (Key West, Florida)

SET 167

Food & Drink	Tate & Lyle
Natural World	Bile
History	Britain
Culture & Belief	Sad
Stage & Screen	Red

Written Word	Len Deighton
Music	Suzi Quatro
Famous People	Frank Sinatra
Sport & Leisure	John Curry
Science & Tech	Tate and Lyle
True or False?	False

SET 168

Food & Drink	Grapefruit and tangerine
Natural World	The Caribbean
History	Elizabeth I
Culture & Belief	A leap
Stage & Screen	Robert De Niro

Written Word	To Kill a Mockingbird
Music	Deliverance
Famous People	Elizabeth Barrett & Robert Browning
Sport & Leisure	Mexico
Science & Tech	Electric and Musical Industries
True or False?	True

SET 169

Food & Drink	Sour cabbage
Natural World	The blue whale
History	Queen Anne
Culture & Belief	Matthew
Stage & Screen	*Frasier*

Written Word	*West Side Story*
Music	Willy Russell
Famous People	Anne Boleyn
Sport & Leisure	Mary, Queen of Scots
Science & Tech	Amelia Earhart
True or False?	True

SET 170

Food & Drink	Pregnant women
Natural World	California
History	The Arts and Crafts Movement
Culture & Belief	S4C (Welsh language TV service)
Stage & Screen	Crane

Written Word	Vito Corleone
Music	*Head*
Famous People	The US Army Air Force
Sport & Leisure	Nadia Comaneci
Science & Tech	Obstetrician
True or False?	False (it is the Czechs)

SET 171

Food & Drink	Mashed turnip
Natural World	The Spey
History	Hong Kong
Culture & Belief	*The War Cry*
Stage & Screen	*Bonanza*
Written Word	Major Major Major Major
Music	Freddie Mercury, Monserrat Caballe
Famous People	Mick Jagger
Sport & Leisure	Diamond
Science & Tech	Diamond
True or False?	False

SET 172

Food & Drink	19
Natural World	Lindisfarne
History	Seaplanes
Culture & Belief	In a grandstand
Stage & Screen	Dr Who
Written Word	Broking
Music	*You'll Never Walk Alone*
Famous People	Iona
Sport & Leisure	Nine
Science & Tech	Glasgow Central and London Euston
True or False?	True

SET 173

Food & Drink	Ultra heat-treated
Natural World	The Andes
History	1936
Culture & Belief	He helped carry his cross to Calvary
Stage & Screen	Three
Written Word	Utopia
Music	*Shake, Rattle and Roll*
Famous People	William Bligh
Sport & Leisure	Diego Maradonna
Science & Tech	1
True or False?	True

SET 174

Food & Drink	Rennet
Natural World	Through their skin
History	Grandson
Culture & Belief	The Apocrypha
Stage & Screen	*Blue Peter*
Written Word	Kurt Vonnegut Jr.
Music	*Blackboard Jungle*
Famous People	Genghis Khan
Sport & Leisure	Both teams sank
Science & Tech	Kitty Hawk
True or False?	False (it was his brother Orville)

SET 175

| Food & Drink | Stale |

| Natural World | Close their eyes |

| History | 1945 |

| Culture & Belief | Flying Squad (Sweeney Todd) |

| Stage & Screen | *Moonlighting* |

| Written Word | Braemar |

| Music | Val Kilmer |

| Famous People | Trafalgar |

| Sport & Leisure | He was the first footballer to be knighted |

| Science & Tech | *The Spirit of St Louis* |

| True or False? | True |

SET 176

| Food & Drink | Barley |

| Natural World | Kentucky |

| History | Franklin D. Roosevelt (1939) |

| Culture & Belief | Shrove Tuesday, or Pancake Tuesday |

| Stage & Screen | *The Man from UNCLE* |

| Written Word | Don Quixote's horse |

| Music | Xylophone |

| Famous People | Dario Fo |

| Sport & Leisure | Lester Piggot |

| Science & Tech | Aspirin |

| True or False? | False (it's 10) |

SET 177

Written Word		John Updike	
Food & Drink	Bouquet garni	Music	*Tubular Bells* by Mike Oldfield
Natural World	Greenland	Famous People	Mathematics
History	*HMS Resolution*	Sport & Leisure	1993
Culture & Belief	November	Science & Tech	The biggest bicycle ever (73 ft long)
Stage & Screen	David McCallum	True or False?	False (it's Greenland)

SET 178

Written Word		A white rabbit	
Food & Drink	Polenta	Music	Denny Laine
Natural World	Monaco	Famous People	Ryan and Tatum O'Neal
History	1970s	Sport & Leisure	Red and green
Culture & Belief	November	Science & Tech	U
Stage & Screen	An Oscar statuette	True or False?	False (it is Lenin)

SET 179

Food & Drink	Apple	Written Word	*The English Patient*
Natural World	Nevada	Music	Little
History	1941	Famous People	George C. Scott
Culture & Belief	Mona Lisa	Sport & Leisure	Croquet lawn
Stage & Screen	None	Science & Tech	*Tron*
		True or False?	True

SET 180

Food & Drink	Garibaldi	Written Word	Harper Lee
Natural World	Staffa	Music	The Tommy Dorsey Band
History	Massachusetts	Famous People	Fred Astaire
Culture & Belief	Hallowe'en	Sport & Leisure	Sporting Lisbon and Sunderland
Stage & Screen	Saxophone	Science & Tech	Aluminium
		True or False?	True

SET 181

Food & Drink	Melba
Natural World	Purple
History	Caernarvon Castle
Culture & Belief	Fire
Stage & Screen	*Cabaret*

Written Word	*Waiting for Godot*
Music	Alexander O'Neal
Famous People	Find Dr Livingstone
Sport & Leisure	Joe Louis
Science & Tech	RADAR
True or False?	True

SET 182

Food & Drink	Pears
Natural World	The Mid Ocean Ridge (in the Atlantic)
History	43
Culture & Belief	Remembrance
Stage & Screen	Dame Judi Dench

Written Word	Sitwell
Music	Jupiter
Famous People	Harry S. Truman
Sport & Leisure	The America's Cup
Science & Tech	Earth
True or False?	False

SET 183

Written Word			*The Young Visiters*
Food & Drink	Grilling	Music	The Rezillos
Natural World	Russian Federation	Famous People	Ireland
History	23	Sport & Leisure	London, Paris or Los Angeles
Culture & Belief	1p	Science & Tech	A nanosecond
Stage & Screen	*Grease*	True or False?	True

SET 184

Written Word			*Treasure Island*
Food & Drink	Peach	Music	The Stranglers (The Guildford Stranglers)
Natural World	Breadfruit	Famous People	The Kennedys
History	1086	Sport & Leisure	42
Culture & Belief	Thou shalt have no other gods before me	Science & Tech	Uranus
Stage & Screen	Quasimodo	True or False?	False (it's the fear of rain)

SET 185

Food & Drink — An alcoholic cocktail or an apple

Natural World — Arran

History — Agincourt

Culture & Belief — 78

Stage & Screen — The Oscar statuette

Written Word — Agincourt

Music — Jim Steinman

Famous People — Confederates

Sport & Leisure — 8 points

Science & Tech — Hydrogen

True or False? — False (he is not on any)

SET 186

Food & Drink — Yes, cream cheese

Natural World — Istanbul

History — Marcus Brutus

Culture & Belief — 16

Stage & Screen — Crete

Written Word — Samuel Beckett

Music — Irving Berlin

Famous People — Lenin

Sport & Leisure — Argentina

Science & Tech — Plastic

True or False? — True

SET 187

Food & Drink	Tomatoes
Natural World	Yangtze
History	George III
Culture & Belief	1984
Stage & Screen	*Cats*

Written Word	Sir John Betjeman
Music	Cello
Famous People	Beheaded
Sport & Leisure	Basketball
Science & Tech	Tupperware
True or False?	False (it's on Bedloe's Island)

SET 188

Food & Drink	Basting
Natural World	Tasmania
History	Bikini
Culture & Belief	Jehovah's Witnesses
Stage & Screen	Jesus and Judas

Written Word	Hilaire Belloc
Music	Hovis
Famous People	B&Q
Sport & Leisure	Chicago Bulls
Science & Tech	Flush toilet
True or False?	True

SET 189

Food & Drink	Largest
Natural World	Barn owl
History	*Titanic*
Culture & Belief	Dance
Stage & Screen	The George Cross
Written Word	Sexton Blake
Music	Maybelline
Famous People	Great-great-grandson
Sport & Leisure	Rod Laver
Science & Tech	Venus and Mercury
True or False?	False

SET 190

Food & Drink	Loaves of bread
Natural World	Wyoming
History	325
Culture & Belief	The meek
Stage & Screen	*The X-Files Movie*
Written Word	American
Music	Ringo Starr
Famous People	Cinema
Sport & Leisure	Mark Spitz
Science & Tech	Red, blue, green
True or False?	True

SET 191

Food & Drink	Easter, Christmas or Mothering Sunday
Natural World	Liffey and Taff
History	Coal
Culture & Belief	Let there be light
Stage & Screen	*Coronation Street*
Written Word	Iain Banks
Music	Charlie Brown
Famous People	Margaret Thatcher
Sport & Leisure	Ski-ing and rifle-shooting
Science & Tech	High fidelity
True or False?	True

SET 192

Food & Drink	108
Natural World	Indian summer
History	Sandinistas
Culture & Belief	16th (1517)
Stage & Screen	He was a horse
Written Word	A fox-hunter
Music	Martin Luther King
Famous People	Martin Luther King
Sport & Leisure	St Leger
Science & Tech	Horsepower
True or False?	False (it was Chicago)

SET 193

Food & Drink	60
Natural World	Anglesey
History	Clothing
Culture & Belief	'Property is theft'
Stage & Screen	*Saturday Night Live*
Written Word	Canada
Music	Bob Geldof
Famous People	Canada
Sport & Leisure	Juan Fangio
Science & Tech	In a brick wall
True or False?	False (it goes around the waist)

SET 194

Food & Drink	Peanuts
Natural World	Ohio, Oklahoma, Oregon
History	Mao Ze Dong
Culture & Belief	Four
Stage & Screen	*Blue Peter*
Written Word	*Daily Express*
Music	Bernard Cribbins
Famous People	Leonid Brezhnev
Sport & Leisure	Betty Stove
Science & Tech	Helicopter
True or False?	True

SET 195

Food & Drink	Tax levied on a barrel
Natural World	St George's Channel
History	Reaganomics
Culture & Belief	Athene
Stage & Screen	The TARDIS
Written Word	Booze
Music	Bernie Taupin
Famous People	In an air crash
Sport & Leisure	American football
Science & Tech	On a £1 coin
True or False?	False (it is the USA)

SET 196

Food & Drink	Choux
Natural World	Yellow
History	6
Culture & Belief	Phylacteries
Stage & Screen	Singapore, Utopia, Zanzibar, Morocco, Rio, Bali, Hong Kong
Written Word	*Barfly*
Music	Paul Weller, Bruce Foxton, Rick Buckler
Famous People	Orson Welles
Sport & Leisure	Brazilian
Science & Tech	7
True or False?	False (it is the sheep)

SET 197

Food & Drink	Fish
Natural World	Mackerel
History	Sri Lanka
Culture & Belief	Mihrab
Stage & Screen	A nickel (5 cents)
Written Word	Harry Potter
Music	Mike Reid
Famous People	Hans Christian Andersen
Sport & Leisure	Evander Holyfield
Science & Tech	3
True or False?	False (it is keys)

SET 198

Food & Drink	Yellow
Natural World	Green
History	BEA and BOAC
Culture & Belief	It no longer says 'new' pence
Stage & Screen	Alexandra Palace
Written Word	J and X
Music	Tuba
Famous People	On a tightrope
Sport & Leisure	Adidas
Science & Tech	Suspension
True or False?	True

SET 199

Written Word	Enemies
Food & Drink	Peru and Bolivia
Music	Humphrey Lyttelton
Natural World	Brazil and Argentina
Famous People	Harry Houdini
History	Nicaragua
Sport & Leisure	New Zealand
Culture & Belief	Epiphany
Science & Tech	Photocopier
Stage & Screen	On the spotlight to direct the beam
True or False?	True

SET 200

Written Word	Philip Marlowe
Food & Drink	Hazelnuts
Music	Wold
Natural World	The Thames (at Oxford)
Famous People	Abraham Lincoln
History	Argentina
Sport & Leisure	Hockenheim
Culture & Belief	2000
Science & Tech	Ohm
Stage & Screen	*Crossroads*
True or False?	False (it was Klapka)

SET 201

Food & Drink	Liver
Natural World	Gibraltar
History	General Galtieri
Culture & Belief	Le Corbusier
Stage & Screen	Ramsay Street
Written Word	William Burroughs
Music	Diana Ross and Lionel Ritchie
Famous People	Le Corbusier
Sport & Leisure	Show jumping
Science & Tech	2
True or False?	False (it was London)

SET 202

Food & Drink	Acetic acid
Natural World	Superior
History	Indira Gandhi
Culture & Belief	Women
Stage & Screen	*Casablanca*
Written Word	*Tales of the City*
Music	50
Famous People	Aristotle
Sport & Leisure	US PGA
Science & Tech	16
True or False?	False (they have four)

SET 203

Food & Drink	Unrefined sugar
Natural World	Hawaii
History	They were not related
Culture & Belief	Fido
Stage & Screen	Oxford, Glasgow and Amsterdam
Written Word	Bob Dylan
Music	Poland
Famous People	Suicide
Sport & Leisure	Kevin Curran
Science & Tech	Hovercraft
True or False?	True

SET 204

Food & Drink	Tapioca
Natural World	Gemini
History	Almost 3 years (2 years 361 days)
Culture & Belief	Duplex
Stage & Screen	Dublin, Glasgow and Sheffield
Written Word	India gained its independence
Music	Number 8
Famous People	Tutankhamun's tomb
Sport & Leisure	Glorious
Science & Tech	*The Flying Scotsman*
True or False?	False (it was 12 seconds)

SET 205

Written Word		Loch Katrine	
Food & Drink	Scurvy	Music	Nat 'King' Cole
Natural World	The Alps	Famous People	Gene Vincent
History	Bangladesh	Sport & Leisure	300
Culture & Belief	On a cheque card	Science & Tech	Galvanised
Stage & Screen	*Monty Python's Flying Circus*	True or False?	True

SET 206

Written Word		Jimmy Durante	
Food & Drink	Wheat (semolina)	Music	*Release Me*
Natural World	From east to west	Famous People	Horatio Nelson
History	Jawaharlal Nehru	Sport & Leisure	Sandy Lyle
Culture & Belief	Thursday	Science & Tech	The solar system
Stage & Screen	Lauren Bacall	True or False?	False

SET 207

Food & Drink	Feta
Natural World	Majorca
History	Charles Stewart Parnell
Culture & Belief	£500
Stage & Screen	Felix (a cat; the others are dogs)
Written Word	Clive James
Music	Funky
Famous People	Henry VIII
Sport & Leisure	India
Science & Tech	Distance
True or False?	False (it is St Andrew's)

SET 208

Food & Drink	Shells
Natural World	Southern
History	Indonesia
Culture & Belief	The Isle of Man's Tynwald
Stage & Screen	*Daktari*
Written Word	*Private Eye* (Richard Ingrams)
Music	Drums and flute
Famous People	Uranus
Sport & Leisure	Harold Dennis Bird
Science & Tech	Kew
True or False?	False (it was Kalinin)

SET 209

Food & Drink	One hour
Natural World	One
History	Spiro Agnew
Culture & Belief	Japan
Stage & Screen	Vietnam, the First World War and the Second World War

Written Word	E. J. Thribbs
Music	Seven
Famous People	Sir Edwin Landseer
Sport & Leisure	Don Bradman
Science & Tech	Singer
True or False?	True

SET 210

Food & Drink	Lancashire
Natural World	Aardvark
History	*Glasnost*
Culture & Belief	Cavaliers & Round-heads (Parliamentarians & Royalists)
Stage & Screen	Mickey Mouse

Written Word	Bill Bryson
Music	16
Famous People	Milan
Sport & Leisure	Ian Botham
Science & Tech	Calico
True or False?	True

SET 211

Food & Drink	Houses of Parliament
Natural World	Herring
History	1961
Culture & Belief	Rampant
Stage & Screen	Eli Wallach
Written Word	Quotations
Music	Elvis Presley
Famous People	Richard Nixon
Sport & Leisure	Surrey (7)
Science & Tech	Shoes
True or False?	False (it was Ecuador)

SET 212

Food & Drink	A slice of lemon
Natural World	Spring
History	1982
Culture & Belief	1801
Stage & Screen	They were brother and sister
Written Word	Topsy (*Uncle Tom's Cabin*)
Music	Jerry Hall
Famous People	1660s
Sport & Leisure	Being out first ball
Science & Tech	Flying saucers
True or False?	True

SET 213

Food & Drink	A gallon
Natural World	Copper and tin
History	The Bay of Pigs
Culture & Belief	St Andrews, Glasgow, Aberdeen, Edinburgh
Stage & Screen	David Jacobs
Written Word	Romeo
Music	Delibes
Famous People	Attlee, Wilson and Callaghan
Sport & Leisure	Essex
Science & Tech	Luddites
True or False?	False (Portuguese)

SET 214

Food & Drink	Orchid
Natural World	Zambesi
History	Roosevelt, Stalin and Churchill
Culture & Belief	Dublin
Stage & Screen	George Lazenby
Written Word	Jane Eyre
Music	Cello
Famous People	Delano
Sport & Leisure	1
Science & Tech	The lines of the hand
True or False?	False (it was York)

SET 215

Food & Drink	X-rays or gamma rays
Natural World	Dogfish
History	Truman, Attlee and Stalin
Culture & Belief	Left a will
Stage & Screen	Berlin
Written Word	The Great Gatsby
Music	Dizzy
Famous People	Sullivan
Sport & Leisure	Lahore, Pakistan
Science & Tech	One gallon
True or False?	False (it's in Switzerland)

SET 216

Food & Drink	Margarine
Natural World	1500ml
History	Churchill
Culture & Belief	Spain
Stage & Screen	Antiques dealer
Written Word	Jane
Music	Tears
Famous People	Crimean
Sport & Leisure	22
Science & Tech	Dentist
True or False?	True

SET 217

| Written Word | Leopold Bloom |

| Food & Drink | Sheep |

| Music | You find a girl to love |

| Natural World | 1953 |

| Famous People | Enrico Caruso |

| History | The Maginot line |

| Sport & Leisure | Joe Davis and Fred Davis |

| Culture & Belief | Gdansk |

| Science & Tech | Water |

| Stage & Screen | Documentary |

| True or False? | False (it was in 1947) |

SET 218

| Written Word | Lord of the Rings |

| Food & Drink | Mozzarella |

| Music | A reason to be cheerful |

| Natural World | One's brother |

| Famous People | Christopher Columbus |

| History | The majority |

| Sport & Leisure | Ray Reardon, Steve Davis, Stephen Hendry |

| Culture & Belief | An officer of the order of the British Empire |

| Science & Tech | Credit cards |

| Stage & Screen | Venice (1932) |

| True or False? | True |

SET 219

Food & Drink	Parma
Natural World	Shipping forecast areas
History	1917
Culture & Belief	Railway workers
Stage & Screen	*Play Misty For Me*

Written Word	Typeface
Music	Two
Famous People	Runcie (all were Archbishops of Canterbury)
Sport & Leisure	Snooker and billiards
Science & Tech	Self-Contained Underwater Breathing Apparatus
True or False?	True

SET 220

Food & Drink	Potato
Natural World	Colorado
History	His severed ear
Culture & Belief	Scotland
Stage & Screen	Ingrid Bergman

Written Word	1954/55/56
Music	Horsehair
Famous People	Oscar Wilde
Sport & Leisure	Tony Jacklin
Science & Tech	By matching fingerprints
True or False?	True

SET 221

Food & Drink	Potatoes
Natural World	Six weeks
History	1938
Culture & Belief	St Francis of Assisi
Stage & Screen	Gene Kelly
Written Word	Garrison Keillor
Music	Green (manalishi/tambourine/door)
Famous People	Natalia Markova
Sport & Leisure	Golf (it's a type of club)
Science & Tech	The sound barrier
True or False?	True (1 January)

SET 222

Food & Drink	Potatoes
Natural World	Salmon
History	Sydney
Culture & Belief	Pali
Stage & Screen	He was the first actor to be knighted
Written Word	Henry Root
Music	(Let's Make Lots of Money)
Famous People	Slavery
Sport & Leisure	Alan Shephard
Science & Tech	Velcro
True or False?	False (it was disobedience)

SET 223

Food & Drink — They're used as a laxative

Natural World — The Fair Isle

History — Clergy, nobility, commoners

Culture & Belief — Scotland

Stage & Screen — Roger Moore

Written Word — He bit off the dog's ear

Music — Steely Dan

Famous People — Liverpool

Sport & Leisure — Golf club

Science & Tech — Ionic and Corinthian

True or False? — False (it wasn't coined until 1966)

SET 224

Food & Drink — Salt

Natural World — Sea horse

History — Hobby horse

Culture & Belief — Switzerland

Stage & Screen — Piccadilly Circus (1896)

Written Word — Iota

Music — Jonathan King

Famous People — Edward VIII

Sport & Leisure — Pancho Gonzalez & Charlie Pasarell

Science & Tech — On a map of the world

True or False? — False

SET 225

Food & Drink	Oil is liquid, fat solid
Natural World	Hudson
History	Rudyard Kipling
Culture & Belief	Limerick
Stage & Screen	1965

Written Word	*Schindler's Ark*
Music	Mott the Hoople
Famous People	1909
Sport & Leisure	Ski-ing
Science & Tech	Nescafé
True or False?	True

SET 226

Food & Drink	Palm tree
Natural World	Bird droppings
History	17th
Culture & Belief	Heroes killed in battle
Stage & Screen	*The Great Dictator*

Written Word	A dance marathon
Music	Sal Solo
Famous People	The Royal Navy
Sport & Leisure	Men's tennis
Science & Tech	The first atomic bomb
True or False?	True

SET 227

Food & Drink	Perrier
Natural World	Dumfries and Galloway
History	Turkey
Culture & Belief	Paul Channon
Stage & Screen	1956

Written Word	1949
Music	*Air on a G String*
Famous People	New York
Sport & Leisure	Arsenal
Science & Tech	Kleenex
True or False?	True

SET 228

Food & Drink	Perrier
Natural World	Stalagmites
History	Kowtow
Culture & Belief	Ottoman
Stage & Screen	Robert Redford

Written Word	Peter Benchley
Music	Buster Bloodvessel
Famous People	Fiji
Sport & Leisure	Bobby Jones
Science & Tech	ra(dio) d(etecting) a(nd) r(anging)
True or False?	True

SET 229

Food & Drink	D
Natural World	Mars
History	The Fabian Society
Culture & Belief	Canada
Stage & Screen	Walter Matthau
Written Word	Two
Music	Matt Bianco
Famous People	Fingal
Sport & Leisure	One
Science & Tech	Hurricane
True or False?	False (that was Joe Louis)

SET 230

Food & Drink	They grow above the ground
Natural World	A mule
History	Robespierre
Culture & Belief	The highwayman had a horse
Stage & Screen	Lassie
Written Word	Inspector John Rebus
Music	David Essex
Famous People	Al Capone's
Sport & Leisure	The Ascot Gold Cup
Science & Tech	Libraries
True or False?	False (every four)

SET 231

Food & Drink	Jennifer Paterson, Clarissa Dickson Wright
Natural World	St Helier
History	Car
Culture & Belief	Sitar
Stage & Screen	Tom Baker

Written Word	William (Willie)
Music	10538
Famous People	Jackie Kennedy
Sport & Leisure	John Spencer
Science & Tech	Architects
True or False?	False (it's a calf)

SET 232

Food & Drink	A can of coke
Natural World	By crushing
History	Man
Culture & Belief	New Zealand
Stage & Screen	Casablanca

Written Word	Humbert Humbert
Music	Jim Croce
Famous People	John Thaw
Sport & Leisure	Policeman
Science & Tech	Bakelite
True or False?	True

SET 233

Food & Drink　Bisto

Natural World　About two years

History　Ford

Culture & Belief　By flea bite

Stage & Screen　The city of Alexandria

Written Word　Tennessee Williams

Music　*With a Girl Like You*

Famous People　Duke of Wellington

Sport & Leisure　Ayr

Science & Tech　A car radio

True or False?　True

SET 234

Food & Drink　Wine

Natural World　A bat

History　Virginia

Culture & Belief　Hallowe'en

Stage & Screen　Bela Lugosi

Written Word　J. D. Salinger

Music　Toto

Famous People　Pope John Paul II

Sport & Leisure　Churchill Downs

Science & Tech　A car

True or False?　True

SET 235

Food & Drink	Almond
Natural World	Leveret
History	1989
Culture & Belief	The Tudor rose
Stage & Screen	Tara King

Written Word	*The Catcher in the Rye*
Music	*It's All Over Now*
Famous People	Edwin (Buzz) Aldrin
Sport & Leisure	The Prix de l'Arc de Triomphe
Science & Tech	*Hamlet*'s 'To be or not to be'
True or False?	True

SET 236

Food & Drink	Neapolitan
Natural World	The Balearics
History	Light emitting diode
Culture & Belief	Plato
Stage & Screen	BAFTA

Written Word	14
Music	*Carmen*
Famous People	Ken Dodd
Sport & Leisure	400m
Science & Tech	New York and Chicago
True or False?	False (it was Jochan Rindt)

SET 237

Food & Drink	Colmans
Natural World	The Solent
History	300 metres
Culture & Belief	The town crier
Stage & Screen	British Academy of Film and Television Arts
Written Word	Tolkien
Music	*Move it*
Famous People	Highgate Cemetery, London
Sport & Leisure	McLaren-Mercedes
Science & Tech	Points of equal depth on sea charts
True or False?	True

SET 238

Food & Drink	Uruguay
Natural World	Ontario and Erie
History	240
Culture & Belief	Jubilee
Stage & Screen	The first Academy Awards (Oscars awards ceremony)
Written Word	The only fruit
Music	Muhammad Ali
Famous People	Woodbine Willie
Sport & Leisure	Brands Hatch
Science & Tech	It was waterproof
True or False?	False (it's three years)

SET 239

Food & Drink	Textured vegetable protein
Natural World	Horseshoe Falls and Rainbow Falls
History	British Telecom
Culture & Belief	£2 coin
Stage & Screen	1700
Written Word	Bertie Wooster
Music	Marie
Famous People	Raffles
Sport & Leisure	Cribbage
Science & Tech	Blood bank
True or False?	False (it was Franz Hals)

SET 240

Food & Drink	Sugar (caramelised)
Natural World	Orkney
History	Spike Milligan
Culture & Belief	Harlequin
Stage & Screen	13½ in (34 cm)
Written Word	Willy Loman
Music	Neil Diamond
Famous People	Ho Chi Minh City
Sport & Leisure	*Bluebird*
Science & Tech	Paper clips
True or False?	True